I0632469

Theodore Child

Wimples and Crisping Pins

Being Studies in the Coiffure and Ornaments of Women

Theodore Child

Wimples and Crisping Pins
Being Studies in the Coiffure and Ornaments of Women

ISBN/EAN: 9783337380021

Printed in Europe, USA, Canada, Australia, Japan

Cover: Foto ©Suzi / pixelio.de

More available books at **www.hansebooks.com**

WIMPLES·AND CRISPING··PINS

BEING·STVDIES·IN·THE
COIFFVRE·AND·ORNA-
MENTS·OF·WOMEN
BY·THEODORE·CHILD
ILLVSTRATED

NEW·YORK
HARPER·AND·BROTHERS
1895

Copyright, 1894, by Harper & Brothers.

All rights reserved.

CONTENTS

ILLUSTRATIONS

"But you will say that hair is but an excrementitious thing."—*Thomas Howell, Familiar Letters.*

Herder, the stupendous German philosopher, compared hair to a sacred forest covering the mysteries of thought. The human body, he imagined, being the type of order *par excellence*, contains in the hair natural disorder similar to the confusion of the hirsute growths of the earth, which are forests.

Monsieur Lefebvre, the eminent capillary artist, in a lecture delivered in Paris in the year 1778, said:

"Coiffure is an art. To modify by agreeable forms those long filaments with which nature seems to have intended to make a veil rather than an ornament; to impart to those forms a consistency of which the matter that composes them does not seem to be susceptible; to give to abundance a regular arrangement that causes confusion to disappear, and to make up for poverty by a wealth which deceives the sharpest eye; to combine accessories with the basis which they are destined to attenuate or to relieve; to strengthen a delicate face by light tresses; to accompany a majestic one by wavy tufts; to redeem the harshness of features or of eyes by a contrast, and sometimes by a purposed harmony; to accomplish all these prodigies without other resources than a comb and a few powders of different colors—such is the essential character of our art.

"The moment he sees a physiognomy the coiffeur must immediately feel what kind of ornament will suit it. A woman, while appearing to have her hair dressed like other women, must nevertheless have it arranged to suit her particular air. Consequently in every toilet the artist is obliged to renew the most difficult of the miracles of Nature, which is to be in all her productions always uniform and always varied."

All this is true. Coiffure is an art, and a great art, the chiefest of the decorative arts, inasmuch as its function is to adorn the most perfect of nature's works, the beauty of woman. Therefore have I ventured to write this little work of reveries and reflections on the dressing of hair and the adornment of beauty, not with a view to superseding the learned theoretical and practical treatises of the masters, nor yet with the purpose of compiling a history of coiffure, but with the more special object of calling attention to the wealth of example and suggestion contained in the paintings and sculpture of past ages, and of thus setting forth indirectly the principles and conditions upon which beautiful coiffure and ornament depend. The documents that have been used in the illustration of these chapters are for the most part the productions of the greatest masters of art, statues and pictures that are the glory of the museums of Europe; but which have perhaps rarely been regarded hitherto in the special light of models worthy of study and imitation by the erudite successors of Monsieur Lefebvre, or as sources of suggestion and inspiration by ladies who are zealous to fulfil their mission of emblems of beauty and visions of comeliness.

Wimples and Crisping-Pins

I

EGYPT

That day Thouboui, a rich young widow of Sân,
was to entertain her friends at a dinner-party.
Her house, situated on the outskirts of the town,
was handsome, and in accordance with her fortune,
but not extravagantly magnificent. Nevertheless,
it was remarkable for the beauty of the paintings
on the walls and ceilings, in which scenes of every-
day life were depicted in bright colors and in ingenious or striking compositions. Thouboui was
also renowned for the fine arrangement of her fish-
ponds, and of her gardens planted with rare trees
and flowers, and adorned with kiosks and alleys
of trellised verdure. She possessed withal many
dogs, cats, tame antelopes, and long-legged rose-
flamingoes, which, in anticipation of the banquet,
were wandering to and fro in the court-yard of
the house, impatiently awaiting the arrival of the

1

guests, whom they proposed to amuse and coax with their familiarities of domestic pets.

The banquet was prepared in a large room or veranda running along one side of the court-yard, decorated with tapestries and hangings curiously woven and embroidered, and furnished with small one-legged tables of precious inlaid woods, arm-chairs, stools, footstools, elegant consoles adorned with bouquets of blue, white, and rose lotus flowers, nepenthes, crocus, and myosotis, sideboards adorned with glass vessels, enamelled pottery, and show - pieces of gold and ivory. Thoubouï was seated in a room preceding the banqueting-saloon, surrounded by her slaves and tire-women, who had decked her with necklaces and bracelets, and with a pectoral composed of several rows of enamelled disks, golden pearls, grains of coralline, and strings of fishes, lizards, and beetles of stamped gold. Her dress, with full sleeves, was of silk, with a large check pattern of carmine and saffron colors, tied with a broad girdle round the waist, and terminating in a flounce of horizontal stripes of the same tints, trimmed with gold fringe, which rustled over her gold-embroidered leather shoes as she raised her feet to allow a slave to pass a cedar-wood footstool. Her long black hair was plaited in innumerable thin triple plaits, the ends of which were tied together in twos and threes with woollen strings. These plaits hung over her shoulders, but were bound together around the head by a fillet of gold braid set with precious stones, while a blue lotus flower hung over her forehead. The shorter hair at the side of the face was interwoven with the longer tresses in two or three plaits, which were tied together at the ends, and allowed to hang down and partly conceal the ear-rings, composed of large single gold hoops. Thus her smooth low forehead, her full brown cheeks, her straight nose, and her finely-chiselled mouth seemed to be presented in a frame, as it were a mirror in a frame of glossy blue-black hair, relieved by the warm scintillations of the gold, the jewels, and the brilliant enamels that decorated the rich ornaments of her bosom. And in the centre of this mirror were two points of dazzling brilliancy, Thoubouï's eyes, the beauty of which was enhanced by the staining of the lids and the blackening of the brows, while the size of the eye was apparently increased by a surrounding ring of kohol, and by the prolongation of the oval with a black line of kohol drawn towards the ear.

Thoubouï, holding a blue lotus in one hand and a copper mirror in the other, looked at her reflected image not without anxiety, for Thoubouï was in love. Her heart yearned towards the young lord Satni, who was to be one of her guests, and her only desire was to please Satni and win his affections. Therefore, not content with the coiffure that her slaves had composed, she called for twenty golden bodkins with spherical heads, which she stuck into her hair above the jewelled fillet. Then taking a kohol-box, which a bronze ape held between his paws, and dipping into the liquid an ivory stick, she proceeded to put more black around her eyes. Then she had bangles in the form of snakes of enamelled gold clasped around her ankles; and on her fingers, the nails of which were reddened with henné, she put many gold rings of various designs, wearing five rings on the third finger of her left hand, and a ring on each thumb.

Thoubouï was now ready to receive, and the tire-women withdrew, while at the same time other slaves brought in chess-boards, and the musicians and dancing-girls took their places in order to be ready when called upon.

Meanwhile the guests began to arrive, some in palanquins and some in carriages, and after slaves had poured water over their hands, and offered to each one a lotus flower, they entered the room where Thoubouï sat, saluted her, took seats, and conversation began, the ladies taking the lead.

And, most of the ladies being of a frivolous turn of mind, the talk at once drifted towards questions of dress. This one would fain know where Thouboui bought her new scarabæus ring, and how much she paid for it. Another was loud in her

GUINEA-HEN HELMET

praises of the head-dress worn at a recent reception by the lady Ra'hel—a sort of helmet in the shape of a guinea-hen, with half-opened wings that covered the temples, while the head advanced over the forehead, forming a lovely *ferronière*.

"This head-dress," continued the lady, "was made by Zedikah, a Hebrew, who has learned to

surpass our native craftsmen in the art of enamelling gold. He is the slave of Petoukhan of Mem-
phis, who made the wedding-crown of Queen Ah-
hotpou. He has imitated the eyes of the plumage
most divinely. Unfortunately, we married women
cannot wear such a coiffure; it is the privilege of
virgins."

"The lady Ra'hel is the favorite of Ammon,"
said Thoubouï, sadly; "her love is requited. Her
wedding with the prince Ennana is announced for
next month."

"Happy Ra'hel!" cried a lady of ripe years,
who was outrageously painted, and dressed with
incongruous ostentation. "Happy Ra'hel! Young
and beautiful, and affianced to a young and beautiful prince, while I am drawing near to the thresh-
old of the good dwelling-place!"

"You are fishing for compliments, fair Nophré,"
said Thoubouï to the lady of ripe years; "you shall
have none until the court-councillor Ahmosis ar-
rives."

"Have you then invited that flower of gentle-
manliness?"

"Do you doubt my friendship?" replied the
hostess. "Should I have invited the bee without
at the same time inviting the blossom? But come!
Let us have some music; and as you, Nophré, have

your thoughts still bent upon amorous exploits, Poeri shall sing us some love-songs."

Thereupon the musicians prepared their harps, guitars, and tambourines, the leader of the melody applied the double flute to her lips, and, at a sign from Poeri, they began to play a plaintive strain composed of a few long-drawn notes, accompanied by the beating of tambourines and the clapping of hands. And Poeri, the beautiful slave, swaying her body voluptuously, began to sing abstractedly, and without enthusiasm. But gradually, as the shrill notes of the flute worked upon her nerves, and the vibration of the tambourines thrilled through her veins, her eyes brightened, her bosom swelled, and, raising her voice, she declaimed in clear tones, joining the words together, and ending each sentence with prolongations and wailing variations upon the last notes:

"Thy love penetrates my heart as wine mixes with water, as perfumes become one with gum, as milk mingles with honey."

Then the double flutes and the harps sounded again, and when they were silent the voice resumed:

"I will lie down in my chamber; I will be sick, and the neighbors will come to ask for news of me. If my beloved comes with them she will put the doctors to shame, for she knows my malady."

Then the double flutes and the harps sounded the intermede, and when they were silent the voice resumed:

"The villa of my beloved has its fountain in front of the house door; the door opens, and my beloved comes out in anger. Oh! that I might become the guardian of her door, that she might give me orders, and that I might hear her voice even when she is very angry and the children are afraid of her!"

Thoubouï, thinking of her passion for Satni, forgot her usual politeness so far as to call for her favorite slave Zari, and order her to sing an elegy of lost love, without asking her guests whether they preferred to hear more music rather than play chess or draughts.

In a brief recitative the singer set forth the situation. The heroine of the song explains to her well-beloved how she has been to set nets to catch the sweetly-perfumed birds of Pount; she asks him to come with her, and prom-

EGYPTIAN LADY

ises him to let him hear the plaintive cries of her beautiful perfumed bird; but her well-beloved refuses, and she therefore abandons the idea of her fowling excursion, and pours out her soul in a tender elegy:

"The cry of the goose sounds plaintive, for it has taken the bait-worm; but thy love repels me, and I cannot free myself from it. I will take away my nets and snares. I will say to my mother, who sees me come home every day laden with captives, 'I no longer set my snares,' for thy love makes me prisoner.

"The goose rises, settles, salutes the granaries with its cry; swarms of birds cross the river, but I no longer pay heed to them; I think of my love alone, for my heart is bound to thy heart, and I cannot depart from thy perfections.

"My well-beloved goes out of his house; he passes without giving attention to my love, and my heart fails within me. In vain do I see cakes and perfumes; in vain do I perceive oils and essences; that which is sweet to the mouth is now bitter for me as gall.

"O my beautiful friend, my desire is to become thy wife and the mistress of thy goods; my desire is that thou walk according to thy will with thy arm laid upon my arm; for then I will

tell to my heart, which is in thy bosom, my suppli-
cations.

"If my great friend cometh not during the night,
I am as one who is in the grave. But thou, art
thou not health and life, art thou not he who trans-
mits the joys of health to my heart that seeks thee?
· "The voice of the turtle-dove is heard saying:
'Behold the dawn. Where is my path?' Thou,
thou art the bird, thou callest me, I have found my
well-beloved in his chamber, and my heart is rejoiced, and I will not escape, but hand in hand I
will walk with thee and be with thee in every
place, happy if my well-beloved make me the first
of women, and break not my heart.

"Ah! let me go out, for behold my well-beloved
cometh towards me. My eyes are fixed on the
ground; my ear listens to the noise of his footsteps
on the road, for I have made the love of my well-
beloved the unique object of desire, and my heart
is never silent when there is question of him.

"But he sends me a messenger, whose feet are
swift to come and to go, to say to me: 'I am not
free.' O thou, whose strength one never tires of
contemplating, why break the heart of another
even unto death?

"My heart is so happy in the hope of thy love
that the front part of my head-dress falls when I

hasten and run to seek thee, and my chignon is in disorder. And yet I assure thee that I adorn my hair and seek to make myself ready to please thee at all hours."

This elegy called forth applause, and the tender chords of the guests having been awakened, Thouboui was encouraged to display the talent of her other singing-women, and, at the suggestion of the sentimental lady Nophré, a song of triumphant love was demanded, and, while dancing-girls as-

EGYPTIAN COIFFURE

sumed attitudes to accompany the words, Poeri recited the "Mirror of the Princess Hathor Moutiritis," as follows:

"A palm of love is the Princess Hathor Moutiritis, a palm among men, a love among women, a palm of love excellent among all women, a maiden whose like has never been seen!

"Black is her hair, blacker than the black of night, blacker than sloes.

"Red are her cheeks, redder than the grains of red jasper."

But before Poeri had finished, Zari broke in with the "Floral Chaplet of Love Triumphant," in which each strophe begins with the name of a plant or flower:

"O purslam, my heart is in suspense when I am in thy arms! I have used kohol to make my eyes more brilliant, and I came close to thee when I saw thy love. O master of my heart, how beautiful is my hour! It is an hour of eternity for me when I rest with thee! My heart yearns towards thee!

"O artemisia of my well-beloved, in whose presence one feels greater, I am thy favorite! To thee I am like the field where I have planted flowers and all kinds of sweet-smelling plants, where I have dug charming canals to cool me when the north wind blows, a delicious place wherein to walk, my hand in thine, with heaving bosom, my heart full of joy at walking together we twain. The sound of thy voice is like strong wine to me, and by hearing it I live: to see thee, and yet to see thee, is of more benefit to me than to eat and to drink!

"O sweet-marjoram of my well-beloved, I took thy garlands when thou camest to me and when thou didst lie down in my alcove. . . ."

At this point a great commotion in the ante-chamber caused the singer to cease, and the attention of all was directed towards the court-yard. Preceded by his footmen, Satni had just arrived in his new curricle, wearing a faultless new wig, and dressed with all the affectation of fashion. Thouboui greeted the young lord with her sweetest smile and her most elegant compliments of welcome, and herself offered him the blue lotus flower which he would hold in his hand during the entertainment. Then, all the guests having arrived, the company repaired to the dining-room; the slaves brought in necklaces of lotus flowers for each one; anointed the hair of the ladies and the wigs of the gentlemen with perfumes and unguents; placed garlands round their heads, and a single full-blown lotus so attached that it hung over the forehead. The beautiful Poeri was charged with anointing and bedecking Lord Satni, and Thouboui bitterly re-

gretted that etiquette did not allow her to accomplish these acts of civility with her own fair hands.
But as the feast advanced the Lord Satni became
very gay and loquacious, and Thoubouï, keeping her
brilliant eyes fixed upon him, half hopeful, half
melancholy, repeated mentally the words of the
" Elegy of Lost Love":

" O my beautiful friend, my desire is to become
thy wife and the mistress of thy goods. . . . The
voice of the turtle-dove is heard saying: 'Behold
the dawn. Where is my path?' Thou, thou art the
bird, thou callest me, I have found my well-beloved
in his chamber, and my heart is rejoiced, and I will
not escape; but hand in hand I will walk with
thee, and be with thee in every place, happy if my
well-beloved make me the first of women, and
break not my heart."

NOTE.—The love-songs intercalated in this sketch were deciphered
by M. G. Maspero from the papyrus of Turin and the papyrus Harris
No. 500.

II

ASIA

THE most ancient moralist that we know, the
Egyptian Ptahhotpou, spoke of women as bundles
of mischief and bags full of lies and wickedness.
The testimony of the wall-paintings of Thebes, of
the bass-reliefs of Louqsor, and of the antique pa-
pyri written by the remote predecessors of Boccaccio and Sacchetti, goes to show that the ladies of
old Egypt, with their plaited hair and jewelled
bosoms, were ardent to attack and weak to resist.
Princesses, daughters of the priestly class, or peas-
ants, all resembled the wife of Potiphar, if we may
believe the ingenious stories, the popular tales, and
the golden legends which have for centuries amused
the ennui of the mummies in their silent tombs,
and which the modern readers of hieroglyphics are
now deciphering for the better comprehension of
the most ancient and perhaps the gayest of civilizations. The Egypt of the Pharaohs is no longer
figured in our imagination as a land of hieratic contemplation, but rather, like our own country, as a

place of joy and of tears, of hopes and of fears, of illusions and emotions—a land peopled by human beings like ourselves, who laughed, sang, loved, and passed. Modern erudition has even succeeded in deciphering love-lyrics that were sung four or five thousand years ago on the banks of the Nile—lyrics in which the ancient Egyptians expressed the sentiments that devoured them—sometimes with exquisite sweetness, at other times with an exuberance and a boldness of imagination that alarm our more sober Western minds. The Egyptian made all nature participate in his amorous emotions— the song of the birds, the perfume of flowers, the murmur of the breeze. Egyptian love is a manifestation of the joyous and splendid harmony of triumphant nature, but at the same time it is tempered by a veil of sadness, and by the ever-present consciousness of the fragility of things and the brevity of bliss.

The Egyptian woman was almost the equal of the man ; she was free to come and go, to tempt and to be tempted, and she made use of her privileges. The land of Potiphar's wife is not the land either of the harem or of the veil. It is in the palaces of Assyria that we must look for the harem. It is in the valleys of the Euphrates and the Tigris, in the cradle of civilization, that we shall find the veil, that emblem of modesty and submission which became one of the arms of coquetry almost as soon as it was invented. The first woman who saw her own image reflected in the still waters of the river, whether Pison, Gihon, Hiddekel, or Euphrates, was the first coquette, and when she began to arrange her hair, to smooth it, to hide it with a veil or shawl, to conceal one part of her face and to reveal another, the art of coiffure was invented.

In the story of Abraham and Sarah we read that when the patriarch sojourned in Gerar, and passed off Sarah as his sister for fear lest the king Abimelech should slay him in order to take her from him, Abimelech, warned by a dream of the wrong that he was about to do, restored Sarah to her husband and gave the two many presents. But before letting them go, Abimelech ironically reproved Sarah, saying, "I have given your brother a thousand pieces of silver, in order that in future, wherever you go, you may always have a veil to wear as a token to all that you are under the lordship of a husband."

A thousand pieces of silver seems a large sum of money to spend on veils, but we may suppose that since Tubal-Cain's sister Naamah first began to stitch her veil with colored threads, the art of weaving fine muslins and precious cachemire had

2

doubtless made great progress, and perhaps already achieved perfection. At any rate, the luxury of fine linen and exquisite tissues is characteristic of the antique Asiatic civilizations. Therefore we may suppose that among the presents which Abraham sent to the daughter of Bethuel—namely, jewels of silver, jewels of gold, and raiment—was included a beautiful veil, the same which she took and covered herself with as soon as she set eyes upon her lord and husband, Isaac, the son of Abraham. From the narrative of the Bible we can reconstitute the scene in all its imposing Oriental simplicity. The caravan, composed of Abraham's servant and his men, and Rebekah and her old nurse, has been journeying for many days. Towards evening they come near the tents, and in the pastures outside the encampment they see a man standing alone and meditating. And the man lifted up his eyes and saw, and, behold, the camels were coming. At the same time Abraham's servant recognized his master's son, and, reining his camel towards Rebekah, he says to the damsel, "Behold my master's son Isaac." Thereupon Rebekah gets down from her camel, and carefully covers her head with a veil in token of submission, modesty, and respect—a symbolism which has been maintained in the bridal costume of the present day.

WOMAN OF OULED NAÏL TRIBE, ALGERIA

In the days of the temporal splendor of the Beni-Israel the habits of patriarchal simplicity were lost. The influence of Egypt and Assyria and commercial relations with the Phœnicians introduced luxury of all kinds ; the veil and the art of embroidery no longer sufficed to adorn the heads of the beautiful Jewesses ; jewels, pearls, and gold and silver ornaments of the richest kind were employed in such abundance that the morose prophets broke forth in threats and imprecations. Thus Isaiah in a passage of precious nomenclature utters terrible menaces :

" Because the daughters of Zion are haughty, and walk with stretched-forth necks and wanton eyes, walking and mincing as they go, and making a tinkling with their feet, therefore the Lord will smite the heads of the daughters of Zion with baldness, and make their bodies naked, so that they shall be ashamed. In that day the Lord will take away the bravery of the tinkling ornaments about their feet, their coifs, their round tires like the moon, the ribbons, the bracelets, the perfume-boxes, the bonnets, the ornaments of their legs, the earrings, the head-bands, the finger-rings, the nose-jewels, the changeable suits of apparel, and the mantles, and the wimples, and the crisping-pins, the mirrors, and the fine linen, and the hoods and the veils."

From this enumeration of objects we see that the
Jewesses frizzled their hair in front and let it hang
down the back in long tresses interwoven with ribbons, or else they curled their hair and let it fall in
ringlets, with a diadem to keep the forehead free,
or a fillet inlaid with jewels, or a net-work of gold,
similar to the coiffure of sequins worn by the Jewesses of the East at the present day. Again, from
the mention of the bonnet or mitra we see that
Assyrian fashions were in vogue, the mitra being a
sort of truncated cone, more or less tall, and enriched with gold, embroidery, and precious stones,
often with a light and rich veil thrown over the
whole. Such a coiffure is worn at the present day
by the Persian and Caucasian women, while among
the Arab tribes, whether in Egypt, Morocco, or Algeria, the fashions in coiffure of thousands of years
ago still persist, with their ornaments of crowns,
turbans, veils, and chains, and all the refinements of
barbaric luxury mentioned by the prophet. Thus,
due allowance being made for facial type, we may
imagine to ourselves the Jewish beauties of old
attired somewhat in the taste of the women of the
Ouled Naïls, whose splendid and exuberant head-
gear is familiar to the modern tourist in Algeria,
and whose chains and turbans and spangled veils
add a singular fascination to the flashing eyes and

the brilliant complexions of the wearers, who, like
Queen Esther, are ruddy through the perfection of
their beauty, which is generally heightened by a
touch of rouge.

Isaiah also refers to the head-bands or precious
stones that hang over the forehead, an ornament
corresponding to the *ferronière* which was so fashionable in Europe during the Middle Ages and the
Renaissance, and which was happily revived during
the Romantic movement in the first half of the
present century. The same beautiful ornament,
frequently seen in the portraits of Leonardo, Mantegna, and the great Venetian painters, is also
spoken of by the prophet Ezekiel in these words
addressed to the personification of Jerusalem:

"I clothed thee also with broidered work, and
shod thee with badgers' skin, and I girded thee
about with fine linen, and I covered thee with silk.
I decked thee also with ornaments, and I put bracelets upon thine hands and a chain on thy neck,
and I put a jewel on thy forehead, and ear-rings
in thine ears, and a beautiful crown upon thine
head."

So too the virtuous Judith braided her hair and
put a tire or mitra upon her head when she started
from Bethulia clad in garments of gladness, wearing bracelets, chains, ear-rings, and all her orna-

ments, decked out bravely to allure the eyes of all
men that should see her, and more particularly to
fascinate the eyes of Holofernes. Likewise Queen
Esther, when she entered the apadana of the great
King Artaxerxes, had spared no pains upon her
toilet, but " being gloriously adorned she took two
maids with her; and upon the one she leaned as
carrying herself daintily, and the other followed,
bearing up her train. And she was ruddy through
the perfection of her beauty, and her countenance
was cheerful and very amiable; but her heart was
in anguish for fear."

Veils, diadems, tiaras, mitras, fillets, crowns;
such are the elements which the art of coiffure
owes to the Asiatics, to those nations who created
the long-vanished splendor of Nineveh and Baby-
lon, those cities of parks and palaces where gen-
erations of proud warriors lived in the ennui of
unlimited luxury and fabulous power. Of Assyrian women, as of the Jewesses who adopted many
of their fashions, we have but very few graphic
records. The Jews, from their fear of the temp-
tations of idolatry, refrained from depicting the
human image. The Assyrians, who confined their
women within the walls of the harem, treating
them as instruments of pleasure whose duty con-
sisted solely in being beautiful and obedient to

WOMAN OF OULED NAÏL TRIBE, ALGERIA

their lord's caprice, covered the walls of their palaces with representations of their exploits in war or in the chase, but appear to have thought their queens and princesses unworthy, or perhaps too sacred, to be exposed to the public gaze even in linear effigy. However, from the magnificence and the complication of the coiffure of the Assyrian men, we may safely conclude that the coiffure of the women was no less magnificent, and in confirmation of this hypothesis we may contemplate a gigantic slab of stone in the Assyrian transept of the British Museum, on which is carved a figure of the winged goddess Ishtar. This figure, discovered by Layard in the Northwest palace of Nimrud, dates from the reign of Asshurnazirpal, 884 B. C., and represents a goddess with four wings, Ishtar or Ashtaroth, holding a necklace, and wearing bracelets, ear-rings, an elaborate series of ornaments on her bosom, and on her head a mitra or bonnet. The hair is waved and frizzed at the ends, while down the back of the goddess hangs a waved switch bound round with a ribbon, below which the hair is frizzed or curled into a ball adorned with two silk tassels.

So we may figure to ourselves Semiramis, the warlike queen, wearing a tall mitra constellated with jewels so brilliant that men's eyes could not

gaze upon it untroubled; so we may imagine her
hair descending in spiral tresses over her scarlet
peplos and glistening with gold-dust, while in each
little curl there lurked a pearl, and at the end of
the torsade an infinite number of diamonds attached to the frizzed hair simulated a nebula of
light — as it were a comet, of which the torsade
was the tail. And over this resplendent coiffure
was thrown a veil of gauze so thin that it seemed
like a light vapor; but yet this veil of mist, far
from dimming the brilliancy of the incomparable
beauty which it enveloped, enhanced it still more,
for the gauze was bespangled with rubies and diamonds so that the sight of it was like the starry
heavens, and the poets compared their magnificent
queen to the shimmering effulgence of the galaxy
whose countless stars no mage has ever numbered.

ISHTAR

III

ATHENS

THE sculptor Euphorion had arrived earlier than usual at his studio in the Street of the Fig Trees, near the Temple of Theseus. It was high midsummer; the heat was excessive, and Euphorion in his uneasy slumber had dreamed that a terrible accident had befallen the bass-relief which he was modelling for the rich Roman collector Lucius Crassus. In his sleep Euphorion had seen the clay begin to steam; then gradually the composition disappeared behind a veil of vapor; and when the vapor vanished in turn there remained of the work nothing but the iron framework or backing of the bass-relief on the stand, and a conical mound of dust on the floor. Such was the force of the heat that it had literally dried and pulverized the modelling clay and annihilated the labor of many weeks.

Euphorion awoke in a cold perspiration, and as the sun was already above the horizon, he girded up his tunic, hurried out of his house, and hastened across the city of Athens to his studio as fast as his legs could carry him. "If by some mischance the dream should prove to be true! What a horrid nightmare!" thought the sculptor to himself as he walked, and from time to time ran, with the early scavenging dogs at his heels as he passed. "Accursed dream of evil omen! Although Glycon of Cos, the Sophist, maintains that we must interpret dreams contrariwise. Perhaps some messenger of the gods, Lord Eros himself, maybe, has come secretly by night to finish my figure. . . ."

Meanwhile Euphorion had reached the end of the Street of the Fig Trees, where his studio was

VENUS OF GNIDOS WITH THE DOUBLE FILLET

situated, and after turning the key with feverish anxiety he flung open the door, and behold the bass-relief was intact, just as he had left it on the previous evening! On the left hand were the two ladies, and on the right Melitta roughly sketched in with the cage full of little Cupids at her feet. Thank Heaven! The dream was but an empty dream.

However, Euphorion proceeded to take the usual precautions. He went out into the garden to draw water from the well, and with a whisk of laurel branches he sprinkled the clay with fresh spray, and carefully placed wet rags on the parts where he had not to work that day. "Let us hope that Lucius Crassus will be pleased," said Euphorion to himself. "The subject is perhaps too amiable, too frivolous, too much in the taste of the day. However, Lucius wishes to have it in terra-cotta, and not in eternal marble. It will be but an ephemeral work, and the Muses will pardon me, seeing that I have done my best. And, after all, I am not responsible if Eros, the great lord of Love, has become the plaything of rhetoricians and story-tellers, and sculptors too, like me, who have to work to please the rich Romans. Let the Muses hold Anacreon guilty, and not me."

"Hail, Euphorion! All hail! May the Muses

guide your chisel, and grant that your servant Melitta may do nothing which is not agreeable, and say nothing but that which is pleasing!"

Euphorion turned with a smile of welcome at the sound of these words of greeting and of suave presage, and replied:

"Hail, Melitta! All hail, most beautiful of Milesian models, and most exact—nay, more than exact, for it is not yet the hour."

"True," answered Melitta, entering the room; "but Cheiron, the baker, told me that he saw you running along the street just now, so I knew that you must be here and ready to work."

"Sweet Melitta, I came in wild haste before the hour because I had a terrible dream this night." And Euphorion related to the girl his strange nightmare, at which she laughed lightly and mocked the sculptor. Meanwhile she took off her petasos—a flat straw hat with a round brim and a little conical crown—untied the fillet that bound her chignon, and let her blue-black hair float over her shoulders.

"How do you wish me to arrange my hair?" asked Melitta, ready to assume the necessary posture as the sculptor might desire.

"This morning," said Euphorion, "we are going to work on the figure of the woman selling Loves.

You must sit on a stool with the cage before you. You have just opened the door and let out one little winged Love. Your costume is good. Your hair must be arranged simply—"

" With a wreath of flowering ivy leaves, like the Muse Thalia?"

" No, no; quite simply."

"Then tied in a bow on the top, with a small chignon on the nape, and tresses over the shoulders?"

" No, that is too ornate even for a seller of Loves. Tie your hair in a simple chignon, with the wavy tresses carried back rather loosely, just covering the tops of the ears, and bound with a double fillet, the coiffure of Kypris and of Artemis, the chaste huntress."

" *The very good and very beautiful goddess*, as the Athenians have engraved on the pedestal of her statue," added Melitta, as she arranged her hair with the aid of a bronze mirror which Euphorion held before her, performing the functions of a handmaiden. " There! One more hair-pin! Ah! Can't I wear a diadem?"

"No, Melitta; respect the purity of the contour of your pretty head. To-day we want neither diadems nor crowns, nor veils nor turbans, nor cylindrical Asiatic coiffures, nor Cypriote curls row

3

THE MUSE THALIA

above row, with high chignon, but simply the
noble and severe Athenian coiffure, which the
great sculptors of old have immortalized."

"You would not have much success as a ladies'

A QUEEN WITH THE CYPRIOTE CURLS

hair-dresser, Euphorion, for I can see that you condemn all the new fashions."

"That is possible, Melitta," replied the sculptor, as he began to work on his bass-relief. With nimble fingers and the enthusiasm of happy labor, Euphorion pursued his task for a long while in silence, and Melitta sat listening to the chirping of the cigales, carefully retaining the pose in which she had been placed. Then, still working with his clay, Euphorion resumed an interrupted train of thought, and said, as much for his own satisfaction as for Melitta's benefit :

"We Hellenes have always been admirers of pure beauty discreetly adorned, but not sacrificed to its own adornment. In the days of the Median wars the Spartans were the finest men in Greece, and their wives and daughters the handsomest women ; indeed, so great was their physical perfection that all the Greeks, even we Athenians, accepted generals from among them without murmuring. The Spartans were the masters of the Hellenes in gymnastics and noble dancing, and although they themselves never excelled in the arts, it is nevertheless to them that we Athenians owe our artistic excellence, more especially our excellence in sculpture ; for without the perfection which gymnastics give to the body we should have had no beautiful models to sculp. Remember the story of Agesilaos, who, in order to encourage his soldiers, had some Persian prisoners stripped before them. When they saw the white and flabby

A VENUS WITH THE BOW

flesh of the Asiatics, undeveloped and unperfected by gymnastics, the Hellenes burst out laughing, and marched onward full of disdain for such an effeminate enemy. Our Hellenic women of old had inborn taste and elegance, and in spite of new-fangled Asiatic fashions, our Athenian ladies—"

"—dye their hair blue, my dear Euphorion," broke in Melitta—" blue like the sky, blue like the sea, blue with rose reflections like the breast of a dove; they powder their hair with gold and white and red; they paint their eyebrows like the Asiatics; they wear their semi-transparent robes like the Asiatics; they curl their hair with irons; they wear nets of golden cords, diadems inlaid with precious stones, wigs, veils, high coiffures. Eu-

phorion, dear master, you are not in the movement."

"And you, Melitta, you are too much in the
movement, for I would wager from the sight of
those dark circles under your eyes that you went
to sup last night with some young lord in company
with Sophists and poetasters and hetairas, your
countrywomen from Miletus."

"You have the power of divination of a Del-
phian seer, Euphorion. I did sup at the house of
Charicles of Alexandria, a rich young stranger who
has lately come to Athens to spend his patri-
mony; at least so says Cleon the Cynic. Charicles
loves the poets and the story-tellers. He has a
beautiful manuscript of the Milesian tales of Aristides."

"And after supper, I suppose, you listened to
that corrupt and frivolous literature?" asked Euphorion, with indignation.

"Yes, dear master," replied Melitta, with win-
ning effrontery, "and we all enjoyed the stories
immensely. Oh! do not be angry. We listened
to some pieces by Meleager also, your favorite
Meleager. Dorothea recited them. Oh! if you
could have seen her, Euphorion, with her hair
floating loose in the Corinthian style, a little cap of
scarlet silk on the top of her head, and a fringe of

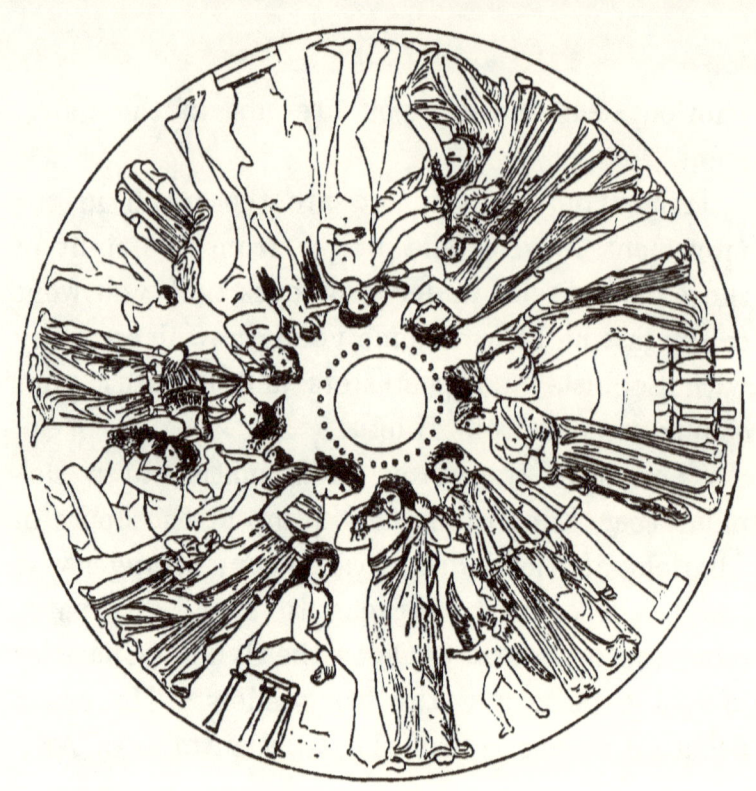

LEKANE FOUND AT KERTCH

gold medallions all round. She looked charming, and she recited some verses that I never heard before. Listen, Euphorion: 'My cup has smiled with joy. Why? Because it has touched the eloquent mouth of Zenophile. Happy cup! Would that its lips might drink up my soul at one draught!'"

"And about his mistress, Heliodora, has Meleager written nothing new?" asked Euphorion.

" Dorothea has received nothing new from her friend, the Tyrian Sebta ?"

" Yes, yes, a sweet madrigal," replied Melitta. "Listen: 'I will wreathe white violets. I will wreathe the soft narcissus with green myrtle. I will wreathe the laughing lily and the suave crocus, the blue hyacinth and the rose dear to Eros, that all may form a crown of beauty to deck the grace of Heliodora's hair.'"

" It is a dainty piece indeed," said Euphorion, approvingly, " and your young lips pronounce becomingly those flowery words. Enough. Let us rest awhile. Here are honey cakes and wine. Go gather some grapes from the vine that shades the doorway, for the noonday heat is fierce, and my hands are slack to mould the clay. Go, Melitta, sweet flower of Miletus."

And Melitta rose from the bench on which she had been sitting, and, taking up her hat, she put it on her head to protect herself from the hot sun. But as she passed she saw on the table a curious lekane, or flat cup with a cover, on which were painted scenes connected with the toilet: a lady dressed, wearing the himation which covers the lower part of her face, is waiting for her companion who is examining her coiffure in a mirror; two ladies who have just been bathing, attended by Loves and tire-women; a young woman, over whose abundant hair an attendant is pouring perfumed water; another woman seated resignedly on a stool while a companion dresses her carefully combed hair; a woman twisting her hair into switches while two others stand and watch her.

"What a beautiful cup!" exclaimed Melitta. "Give it to me, Euphorion, and I will be your model for a year—for two years!"

"Alas, Melitta, it is not mine to give. It is an antique cup three hundred years old, which Lucius Crassus bought when he was in Athens last spring. He left it in my care, together with this perfume-bottle in the form of Aphrodite Anadyomene rising from the sea."

Melitta took the bottle in her hands, admired the cordon of pearls passing over the bosom of the figure, the rich necklace, the crown with its gilt rosettes placed so delicately on the curled hair, the dark blue of the eyes, the gold of the crown, of the hair, and of the necklace, and, above all, the red of the inside of the shell setting off the roseate pearliness of the flesh.

"Oh, Euphorion, what an exquisite bottle! Would that it were mine! Would I were rich! How happy must she be who enjoys the favor of Lucius Crassus!"

With a sigh and a wistful look at the precious
objects, Melitta went forth to gather grapes, and
when she returned she sat down in silence, and

APHRODITE ANADYOMENE

dreamily nibbled a honey cake in front of Euphorion. After a while Melitta, looking shyly at
the sculptor, said,

"Lucius Crassus is coming back to Athens soon, is he not?"

"Yes; on his way from Alexandria to Rome."

"From Alexandria? Then perhaps he knows Charicles?"

"Doubtless."

"He will go to sup with Charicles. I shall see him, perhaps. Oh, if I only had beautiful apparel, some Tyrian veils, and a jewelled diadem like Dorothea!"

"Melitta, you are allowing your mind to revel in the romantic intrigues dear to Aristides the Milesian. I read your thoughts. I divine your vaulting ambition. You would fain set the snares of your young beauty in the path of Lucius Crassus. For shame, Melitta, for shame!"

"Pardon, Euphorion," replied the blushing Melitta. "I was but joking."

"Nay, so was I joking too, Melitta. Go your wanton ways, and may Kypris and Eros protect you. Life is but a span. Be gay, be joyous and happy while you may, for, as the poet says:

"'Short is the rose's bloom; another morn
No rose is there: you find instead a thorn.'"

IV

ROME

It was in the spring of the year A.D. 208. Tertullian had recently bidden farewell to the brethren in Carthage, his native town, and had settled in Rome, with a view to taking part in the controversy between the partisans of Praxeas and those of Montanus that was then agitating the Roman Church. For the moment, however, he had not declared himself, although he had no hesitation in sympathizing with the rigidly ascetic principles of the Montanists, rather than with the lax and indulgent views of those who were not disposed to look upon the world as a monastic association, or upon the practice of Christianity as a perpetual struggle against human nature. Meanwhile the great polemist, comfortably lodged in the house of a deacon of the Church, Proxenes, who in former years had been a steward in the employ of the good emperor Marcus Aurelius, was reading the epistles of St. Paul and making notes for one of his minor treatises, *De Cultu Feminarum*.

The first battle was about to be fought between Christian piety and the spirit of worldliness, between monasticism and society, between renunciation and the joy of living. Tertullian, accustomed as he was to the luxury of Carthage, had nevertheless been scandalized by the still greater luxury of Rome, and especially by the splendor of the costume and the personal ornaments of the Roman ladies, whose example appeared to him to be exercising a disastrous influence upon many Christian women. Therefore the moment seemed to him opportune

DANCING-WOMAN WITH SIMPLE FILLET

to determine once for all what was the becoming costume for Christian widows, deaconesses, wives, and virgins, and with this object he was copying his texts. First of all, the precepts of St. Paul in his Epistle to Timothy, where he says that Christian women should adorn themselves "in modest apparel, with shamefacedness and sobriety; not with broidered hair, or gold, or pearls, or costly

array"; and then the passage in the Epistle to
the Corinthians, where St. Paul requires Christian
women to wear their hair covered with a veil, saying: "Judge in yourselves: Is it comely that a
woman pray unto God uncovered? Doth not even
nature itself teach you, that if a man have long
hair, it is a shame unto him? But if a woman have
long hair, it is a glory to her; for her hair is given
her for a covering." Finally St. Paul, in order
to cut short all objections, states categorically that
the Church insists upon women being veiled. It is
not the Christian custom, he says, for women to
wear their hair uncovered. "But if any man seem
to be contentious, we have no such custom, neither
the churches of God."

The traditions established by the early Christians
restored the use of the simple opaque veil, forming
a sort of hood in place of any complicated architecture of plaits and chignons, and it was generally
accepted that matrons must wear veils in church
and in all religious assemblies. On the other hand,
the girls and the unmarried women seem to have re-
belled instinctively against a custom which obliged
them to hide a portion of the arms of beauty.
Hence arose the question of the veiling of virgins, which Tertullian was about to treat. And
taking up his tablets, he began to compose his

argument, beginning with a vigorous reprimand of those weaker sisters who were worldly enough to disregard the precepts of St. Paul and who refused to wear veils. "They abandon the head-dress of childhood," he wrote, "but only to consult their looking-glasses, to soften their skin with essences, and perhaps even to paint their faces. They wear mantles and different kinds of shoes, and they have altogether the look of married women, except that they wear their hair without the covering of a veil, in order to display the elegance of their coiffure and captivate the eyes of men. But the mind of a virgin ought not to be concerned with pleasing men. At every age there is danger. Clothe yourselves with the arms of modesty; fortify yourselves with the rampart of modesty; surround your head with a wall that will guarantee you against the attacks of others."

Tertullian paused and read over what he had written, but without satisfaction. True these were but notes which his ardent African eloquence would vivify and adorn with sharp touches. He would speak also of the error of the married women, whose irrepressible coquetry had invented caps and diminutive bonnets of fine linen, which they wore instead of the real veil that covers and conceals the hair. Nevertheless, Tertullian felt

DANCING-WOMAN WITH RINGLETS IN FRONT

that his brain was heavy, and that his prose did
not flow easily. The literary man began to criti-
cise the polemist. The brilliant pupil of the rhetoricians of Carthage reasserted himself in the person
of the grave and ascetic doctor. The subject of
woman and the ornaments of woman had sufficed
to fill him with a desire to treat it with gracefulness of language and with all the art of the accom-
plished rhetorician, for in reality Tertullian, mighty
genius, vigorous thinker, and vehemently ascetic
Christian as he was, remained throughout his life
an incorrigible man of letters, a literary artist
delighting in ingenious metaphors, refined erudition, and subtle phraseology.

And so Tertullian began to reflect, and to recall
to mind the methods and precepts of the literary
schools of Carthage, whereas in similar circum-
stances a Christian doctor of less scholastic training
would have simply prayed for inspiration, or merely
plodded along in a commonplace but sincere argument. The more Tertullian thought about his subject, the less ascetic his thoughts became, and the
stronger his curiosity. "In order to present my
argument vigorously," he reasoned to himself, "I
must be armed with instances; I must have an
abundance of recent observation; I must refresh
those souvenirs of worldly frivolity which I ac-

4

quired in the days when I was still unregenerate. I will go and take a walk through the streets and observe the fashions, so that my prose will gain in color and sharpness. I need a good deal of description in this treatise."

Tertullian laid aside his tablets and started to go out, but at the door of the house he met his host, Proxenes, and being yet unfamiliar with the habits of Roman society, he explained to him his embarrassment and asked for advice. Where could he see the fashionable ladies? Where could he conveniently get information about the artifices of coiffure and toilet?

Proxenes, whose ascetic ardor was less violent than that of Tertullian, and whose attitude towards the pagans was conciliatory rather than aggressive, gave the Carthaginian doctor some hints for his guidance through the streets, and gradually becoming himself interested in the subject, he bethought himself of a man who would be of the greatest use to Tertullian, one Apicius Naso, formerly jeweller to the Empress Faustina, and one of those professors of hair-dressing who trained the slaves of the rich Roman ladies, and taught them the theory and practice of coiffure. Naso, now advanced in life and wealthy, had remained deeply interested in the arts to which he owed his fortune. Although

EMPRESS FAUSTINA

practising the ancient religion, he was a good and gentle man, liberal-minded, a Platonist in philosophical opinions. Proxenes had known him when he was in the service of Marcus Aurelius. If Tertullian had no objection, Proxenes would introduce him to Naso.

Tertullian accepted the offer with joy, and the doctor and the deacon hastened through the crowded streets, crossed the river, and pursued their way to a villa in the outskirts of the city, where Apicius Naso lived in a forest of roses. The old jeweller welcomed Tertullian to his home with every mark of honor, saying that he should feel greatly flattered to show his frivolous collection of feminine ornaments to so profound a scholar and so pious a teacher of virtue.

Thereupon Apicius led the way into a long gallery lined with pedestals, on which were placed marble busts of famous Roman ladies, the flesh and the draperies delicately tinted, while the hair and the ornaments were likewise colored discreetly. There was the Empress Faustina, the wife of Antoninus Pius, wearing an exquisite coiffure of waved hair, a simple fillet, and a high-placed chignon of braids coiled on the crown ; Didia Clara, with low chignon and hair waved in the Greek style ; Julia, daughter of Titus, with a high chignon and a mass of little curls surrounding the forehead; the same Julia with a round chignon of plaits, a tall frontal of small curls rising like a diadem above the head, small regular curls round the forehead, and in front of each ear three small ringlets. Julia Aquilia Severa, with her hair parted in the middle and falling in heavy loops, caught up and tied over the nape; Domitia, with her hair frizzled into an infinite number of curls all over her head; a head of Juno, with waved hair, a diadem, a chignon, and a string of amber beads passing in front of the diadem and falling behind the ears, with ringlets coiled around; and many other busts with beautiful or eccentric coiffures, while at the end of the gallery were two statues of dancing-women, one with short ringlets and a simple fillet binding the head, and the other with short ringlets in front and long ringlets behind, the head being likewise bound with a fillet. All these busts Tertullian examined with curiosity, as Apicius, playing with a ball of pure rock-crystal, that he used in the Eastern manner to keep his hands cool and fresh, explained to him the characteristics of the coiffure; the manner of setting the diadems in the hair; the different systems of plaiting, curling with irons, waving and frizzling hair; the methods of making bows of hair

JUNO

and of interweaving plaits with strings of pearls; the various shades of blond and red hair which came into fashion after the conquest of the Germans; the caustic soap and dyes used to change the color of the hair; the manufacture of wigs and false chignons, and the fickleness of fashion. In proof of this latter phenomenon, Apicius called the attention of Tertullian to the fact that the coiffure of several of the busts in his collection was movable, so that when the fashion changed a new coiffure could be substituted in place of the old one, and the lady be spared the grief of seeing a portrait of herself not absolutely *à la mode*, or so obviously old-fashioned that it would give disastrous information regarding her age. Finally, Apicius pointed out the bust of a lady tastefully veiled, with just a little of the hair visible around the forehead, a concession to coquetry which matrons sometimes abused. "This coiffure, with a veil completely concealing the hair and falling over the shoulders, is that of the Vestal Virgins," added Apicius. "It is the ideal Roman coiffure, and the model which the typical Roman matron affects to imitate."

Apicius then showed Tertullian a series of combs of box-wood and of ivory daintily carved, various kinds of curling-irons, and many models of long hair-pins used to hold the coiffure in position, some of them having a hole at each end, through which the fillet was passed and tied. The heads of these pins were curiously chiselled in the form of figures and groups of Venus and Cupid, Cupid and Psyche, Isis, and other subjects. Apicius showed one pin which was a hollow tube destined to contain poison, and remarked with a smile that, as a collector, he would be glad to believe that this was the pin with which Cleopatra poisoned herself, but, as a jeweller, he was unable to forget that he had had the pin manufactured for a Corinthian hetaira, who had left it on his hands.

Apicius next opened a case of drawers, in each of which was a mirror of polished metal, the mirror side of silver, the back of gold chased in admirable designs and set around with precious stones. Then he showed toilet-cases in silver, fans, bracelets, necklaces, cameos, ear-rings, and ornaments of gold, explaining the variations of Roman taste in jewelry, and affirming his conviction that in the matter of ornaments, as of coiffure, the true models were to be sought in the inventions of the Athenians and the Corinthians; "for our Roman ladies," he said, "though insatiable in the pursuit of novelty and ingenious in the imagination of luxury, are not always remarkable for their artistic taste."

VESTAL VIRGIN

After some further talk with Apicius about the luxury of women, Tertullian and Proxenes took leave of the amiable specialist, and returned through the city, both the doctor and the deacon feeling their powers of observation mightily sharpened, so far as concerned feminine elegance, by the explanations and illustrations which Apicius had submitted to them. Tertullian stopped to look in all the shops where ladies' ornaments and attire were displayed, and Proxenes from time to time, good deacon as he was, could not refrain from marvelling at the splendor of some beauty or another that passed them, reclining in a litter borne by Cappadocian slaves. Proxenes even ventured to suggest to Tertullian that it would be a hard thing for the Church to conquer the luxury of the world, and that perhaps the Church would make more proselytes by indulgence than by rigorism. But the Carthaginian was so absorbed in his literary reflections, and in the mental trituration of all the observations that he had just made, that he did not combat the backsliding opinions which Proxenes had expressed, but, answering him evasively, hurried along, and as soon as they reached the house thanked Proxenes, retired to his room, and resumed his polemical prose with renewed ardor at the point where he had left it a few hours before. And as

Apicius's remarks about paint and hair-dyes and their consequences were uppermost in his mind, he proceeded to write:

"I see some women who are all the time occupied with applying washes to their hair to give it a blond color. They seem to be almost ashamed of their father-land, and to blush with regret because they were not born in Gaul or Germany. A sad presage is this coiffure, a vain and gloomy beauty which at last ends in ugliness. Is it not true that by the use of these washes and perfumes women gradually lose their hair? Is it not a fact that their brains are affected by these strange lotions, and by the excessive heat of the sun to which they expose their hair to dry it? A Christian woman makes her head a sort of altar, on which she pours libations of perfumery in profusion.

"'See,' they say, 'how we change white or black hair into blond, so that it may look more beautiful'; and there comes a time when they spare no pains to change their white hair into black when they have reached fatal old age, and are full of desolation because they have lived too long.

"Of what avail for salvation is this wearisome care that you take to adorn your head?

"What! Cannot you leave your hair in peace? At one time you are curling your hair, at another

JULIA, DAUGHTER OF TITUS

you are uncurling it. At one time you are lifting
it up, and at another you are letting it down. One
day you braid your hair, and the next day you let
it float over your shoulders with affected negligence;
and then another day you load your head with an
enormous heap of false hair, which you arrange in
the form of a bonnet to imprison your head, or in
the form of a pyramid so as to show the neck uncovered. No one, says Jesus Christ, can add anything to what he is, and yet you would add something by piling up on your head tufts of hair loaded
with ornaments like the boss of a shield. If you
do not blush through the weight of this burden, at
least you must blush for its unworthiness. Do not
place upon a head that has been sanctified by bap-
tism the remains of some wretch who has died in
debauchery, or of some criminal who has expiated
his crimes on the scaffold. May it please God that
on the day when the Christians triumph, I, unworthy as I am, may be permitted to raise my
head to your proud height, that I may see if you
come to life again with your paint, your rouge,
your perfumes, and your superb hair."

At this moment Proxenes came into the room,
followed by his daughter Priscilla, who carried
on a tray the frugal repast, which was all that
the austere Tertullian allowed himself—bread, len-

tils, cheese, and fruit. And Proxenes held a manuscript in his hand, the Book of Enoch, and respectfully begging the permission of his illustrious guest, he called his attention to the enumeration of the chiefs of those angels who united themselves with the daughters of men, and begot giants, each three hundred cubits high. "These giants devoured all the work of man, until they could not be satiated," read Proxenes from his scroll. "Then they turned against men to devour them. And they began to put to death beasts, reptiles, and fish, and to eat their flesh and drink their blood. Then the earth reproved the unjust. Azaziel taught men to make swords, shields, and corselets; he taught them to make mirrors and bracelets and ornaments, and the usage of perfumes, and of precious stones of all colors. Impiety increased, shamelessness waxed greater, and all transgressed and walked in the path of corruption."

"Yes, my good Proxenes," answered Tertullian, "the only garment that befits woman is mourning, for it was through woman that sin came into the world; and you, Priscilla, beware of the evil example of those of your sex who walk about with their heads uncovered, and wear silk dresses with many plaits that rustle as they walk, who have their necks adorned with many rows of pearls, and

DIDIA CLARA

their arms decked with bracelets like the pagan priestesses of Bellona and Ceres. Hands that are accustomed to bracelets are not strong to bear the weight of chains. Legs that have been swathed with bands of silk will scarcely be able to endure the pain of shackles. A head covered with emeralds and diamonds will, I fear, bow basely beneath the sword of martyrdom with which we are threatened at every hour."

V

THE MIDDLE AGES

The object desired in the arrangement of hair may be either beauty or richness, artistic comeliness or barbaric splendor, charm obtained by means of the elements which nature provides, or magnificence due to the profusion of extraneous ornaments. The most admirable coiffures of the Greek and the Roman civilizations are the simplest. The natural chignon, the waved hair bound with a narrow fillet, or at the utmost adorned with a diadem — such is the ideal and such the artistic standard to which fashion returns century after century, whenever its vagaries become excessive and end in ridicule or inconvenience. The progress of fashion is from too little to too much, from simplicity to extravagance, from no ornament at all to ornament that overpowers everything else. The moment an ornament comes into use its importance begins to grow, and continues growing until its luxuriance overwhelms and entirely conceals what it was originally intended to adorn. One jewel in the hair attracts another and another; a golden diadem invites a crown, and a crown suggests a helmet enriched with diamonds and precious stones; even the veil, the emblem of modesty, destined to conceal, is made a flag and a banner of coquetry, and in its various and innumerable transformations it becomes wimple, turban, coif, or bonnet, and in the end a mere pretext for ornamentation.

The contrast with the artistic simplicity of Greek and Roman fashion is furnished by the stiff garments of heavy silk embroidered with pearls, precious stones, and ornaments of gold and colored glass which were invented by Byzantine taste, and by the prodigious coiffures worn by the Empress Theodora and her suite, as depicted in the famous mosaics of Ravenna. Byzantine fashion left scarcely any hair visible. The head was loaded with pads and rolls of rich stuffs embellished with pearls and precious stones, on the top of which were worn heavy crowns with pendeloques of pearls. The neck and bosom were loaded with chains of gold enriched with precious stones. The very shoes were embroidered with pearls. In short, Byzantine taste, which is generally considered to be bad taste, carried to the extreme point the research for splendor and magnificence, and dressed women to look like Oriental idols. Nevertheless, it must not be forgotten that in the civilization of modern Europe Byzantine art played a great and beneficent rôle; it inspired and guided that taste for luxury and that desire of beauty which produced the architecture of mediæval Italy, and gave consciousness to the artistic Renaissance in the time of Charlemagne.

The history of hair-dressing in Europe begins with long tresses floating over the shoulders and held in place by a simple head-band. The next step is the division of the tresses by a parting, and the plaiting and lacing of each switch with ribbon so that it forms a rope. These two ropes may hang in front of the wearer, or over the shoulders and down the back. Then, again, the two switches produced by the parting may be gathered into one long braided pigtail, as is shown in the accompanying illustration, which is a portrait of a lady by Piero della Francesca (1415–92). Furthermore, the two primitive switches may be coiled up or otherwise arranged at the sides, at the back, or on the top of the head. Finally, ornamentation is obtained by the development of such elements as are contained in veils, coifs, jewels, and crowns.

The picture by Piero della Francesca, although it is of the fifteenth century, will serve perhaps better than more archaic works to explain the

PORTRAIT OF A LADY, BY PIERO DELLA FRANCESCA

progression above indicated. Let us see how this coiffure is executed. First of all, the hair is parted in the middle of the head, and so hangs in flowing tresses like a veil over the shoulders and back. If the coiffure were destined to remain thus, some fillet, circle, or diadem would be needed to keep the hair in place and prevent it falling over the eyes. Hence the crowns or "chapels," used by both men and women, which we see represented in mediæval sculpture and in the miniatures of the twelfth, thirteenth, and fourteenth centuries. As for the crowns, properly so called, they were worn in the Middle Ages by kings, princes, and counts only, and their form varied according to the fancy of the maker and the wearer, there being no difference between men's crowns and women's crowns except in size. The heraldic crowns, such as they are classed nowadays, were not formally distinguished until the sixteenth century. Girls, both noble and other, and those women whose rank did not allow them to wear crowns, wore gold or silver circles, either of plain metal or else enriched with enamel, precious stones, or ornaments. Furthermore, the use of crowns of natural flowers, common to Greek and Roman antiquity, persisted until the time of the Renaissance, as we read in the romance of Lancelot, who wore

5

a chaplet of fresh roses on his head every day of
the year except on Fridays and on the eve of great
fêtes, "il ne fut jour où Lancelot, ou hiver ou été,
n'eust au matin un chapel de fresches roses sur la
teste, fors seulement au vendredi et aux vigilles
de hautes festes." This custom suggested to the
goldsmiths a dainty device for "chapels," whereby
they wrought flowers of gold, which were sewn
on a band of ribbon or galloon. Precious stones
and jewels, too, were sewn on galloon in like manner, and so the "chapel" of the lady depicted by
Piero della Francesca is composed of a narrow
fillet of velvet, to which are attached thirteen ame-
thysts, one of which occupies the centre of her
forehead. Finally the fillet was shorn of all ornament except one precious stone or jewel, which it
served merely to fix in the centre of a limpid brow.
Thus in Mantegna's portrait of the Duchess Eliza-
beth Gonzaga we see in the centre of the forehead
a jewelled scorpion, emblem of logic, while a similar isolated jewel is worn by Lucrezia Crivelli in
her portrait in the Louvre by Leonardo da Vinci,
commonly known as "La Belle Ferronnière"—
the name of a "chapel" of this kind being in
French *ferronnière*. The usage of the *ferronnière*
was revived in the beginning of the present century, when the Romantic movement in art was at

its height, and a charming example is given in
our illustration, engraved from an exquisite lith-
ograph by Grévedon (1783–1849). The lady portrayed by Grévedon wears her *ferronnière* high
on account of the chignon, the position of which
necessarily determines the inclination of the fillet or circle. The fillet, too, is rather wide.
With a low chignon the fillet would bind the head
horizontally, and the jewel would then fall in the
centre of the forehead. However, the usage of
the *ferronnière* seems to be thoroughly consecrated
by the traditions of adornment of beauty, and it
is strange that the women of the present day have
rarely ventured to revive the fashion. On the
other hand, it is true that piquant and unquiet
beauty could not wear a *ferronnière*. This ornament requires calm and regular features and dignity of gesture and attitude; it is the ornament
of that fair bride of whom Matthew Arnold says:

> " On her front did glow
> Youth like a star ; and what to youth belong—
> Gay raiment, sparkling gauds, elation strong."

But to return from this digression to the portrait by Piero della Francesca. Having parted
the hair, and left the front tresses sufficiently loose
to cover the ears, we tie the two switches together

above the nape of the neck, and proceed to plait the pigtail and bind it round with ribbons. Then, in order to hide the parting at the back of the head, we place a little coif of richly embroidered samite, constructed on a wire frame, and adorned with two heavy jewels and droppers, which take the place of ear-rings. These jewels were perhaps mounted on pins, which would in that case serve to hold the coif in position, in addition to the circle or "chapel" that completes the coiffure. In the embroidered cap and the rich jewelry used in this example we remark the remnants of Byzantine influence, which became so powerful in Europe in the twelfth century, when the crusades placed the West into close and constant communication with the East, and brought into fashion the rich tissues and elaborate ornaments not only of the Byzantines, but also of the Arabs.

Another portrait by Piero della Francesca, that of the Duchess of Urbino, in the Uffizi Gallery at Florence, will enable us to comprehend the arrangement of the primitive switches at the sides of the head. This coiffure is simple in theory, but somewhat complex in execution. First of all the short hair at the edge of the cheeks is reserved and carefully curled with an iron. The long hair is parted in the middle and behind so as to form

A LADY WITH A FERRONNIÈRE

two switches, one on each side, and each switch is bound round with ribbon, the end alone being left loose. The switch thus bound is coiled and fixed with a brooch, behind which the loose end floats. The division of the hair obtained in this way leaves a parting visible at the back of the head, and in order to conceal this feature, and also in order to re-establish the contour destroyed by the displacement and compression of the volume of hair, a veil is fixed so as to form a sort of artificial chignon and to fall over the neck. Finally, a rich jewel, like a diminutive crown, is attached on the top of the head to a ribbon, which appears to pass behind the ears and be connected with a fine cord that is seen under the lady's chin. Every detail of this coiffure is rich and rare, and the ensemble is worthily completed by the magnificent carcanet and pendant of precious stones that clasps the neck and falls over the bosom.

To follow the transformations of the veil which was so strongly recommended by St. Paul and Tertullian would lead us into endless developments. The theme is, indeed, curious and interesting, and those who would write a complete history of coiffure need to study it with minuteness. Such, however, is not our object; we have no preten-

sions to write a history of coiffure, but merely to
select from artistic monuments examples of coiffure and ornament that remain stamped with the
eternal imprint of style; our business is with what
is beautiful rather than with what is curious, and
our design is to present to the fair reader not the
results of archæological research, but the suggest-
ions for elegance contained in visions of feminine
beauty and character selected from among the
great works of the art of the past. In the history
of feminine coiffure there is to be noted a perpetual and inevitable hostility between the ornament
and the thing adorned, between the hair and the
veil and its developments, between the natural
elements of coiffure and the artificial elements.
The tendency of ornament is to spread and monopolize. The veil, destined to conceal, is gradually made transparent, and finally abolished, until one day it reappears in a diminutive and
insidious form, and once more grows and grows,
until its monopoly has yet again to be destroyed,
and the hair delivered from its prison-house. Thus,
in the Middle Ages, the veil in the form of *men-
tonnières, gorgières*, and *guimpes* gradually enkerchiefed the hair, and concealed it entirely, produc-
ing, on the one hand, those close coiffures of which
the souvenir remains in the costume of the various

THE DUCHESS OF URBINO

orders of nuns and sisters of mercy, and, on the other hand, the voluminous *escoffions* and the high-peaked *hennins* or steeple head-dresses, which formed as it were rich cushions and gay masts, whereon floating veils were displayed and rigged. Yet other developments of the veil are nets, which were used for centuries in ancient Rome, and revived in the fashions of the Middle Ages. We may even venture to consider the capuchon or hood to be a development of the veil, for in its simplest form the hood is a primitive veil or mantelet tied round the neck under the chin so as to protect the head. Evidently we could call attention to innumerable forms of hoods, *hennins*, and *escoffions* that are quaint, amusing, graceful, and even suggestive; but with few exceptions these coiffures are so exceptional, so ephemeral, and generally so eccentric that the study of them would lead us away from our subject into the too fascinating domain of archæological curiosity. It will suffice for us to remember that the veil and the hood have finally gained semi-independence, and that nowadays, in the form of hats and bonnets, they are the province of the milliner rather than of the hair-dresser proper. While formerly the coiffure of a lady was essentially the same in-doors and out-doors, nowadays a lady, when she goes

out, adds to her ordinary coiffure the additional
ornaments which her milliner provides. The
Duchess of Urbino walked in the streets with her
hair dressed as we see it in her picture. The lady
with a pigtail, whose portrait we have reproduced,
also went abroad with no other head-gear than her
diadem and her embroidered cap, which is, however, an embryo bonnet. But a hundred years
later the two girls whom Bernard van Orley
(1490–1560) painted at prayer with their mother, as we see in a grand picture in the Brussels
Museum, wore regular bonnets, which would require small change in order to adapt them to the
modern taste.

PORTRAIT OF TWO GIRLS, BY BERNARD VAN ORLEY

VI

FLORENCE

In his famous book *The Courtier*, that flower of
sixteenth - century culture, the Count Baldassar
Castiglione maintains that the courtier, or, as we
should now say, the well-educated man or the perfect gentleman, ought to have some skill in painting, not only because it is a noble art, attended
with much credit and advantage, but because it
helps him to judge of the excellency of statues,
both ancient and modern, of vessels, buildings,
medals, engravings, and such like, and, above all
things, because it gives him a better taste and
knowledge of living beauty, not only in the sweetness of the countenance, but in the just proportion
of all the parts, as well in men as in all other animals. "You see, then," continues our author,
" that the knowledge of painting is the occasion of
an infinite deal of pleasure, which they may frame
some guess of who view and enjoy the beauty of
some fair one to that degree that they imagine
themselves in Paradise; and this without the

knowledge of painting, which had they but acquired, it would mightily enhance their satisfaction; for then they would more perfectly understand the beauty which raises such pleasing transport in their breasts."

This excellent advice applies to the adornment of beauty as well as to beauty itself. A knowledge of painting, and more particularly a knowledge of the noblest pictures that the world has produced, mightily enhances the satisfaction of those who delight in the adornment of beauty, because it enables them more perfectly to understand and more successfully to pursue their ideal. As beauty is a gift worthy of sedulous cultivation, so is the adornment of beauty a subject that demands and repays minute study; and the best text-books in which such study may be made are surely statues and pictures, for none have devoted more thought and invention to adorning the beauty of women than sculptors and painters. As there are several sorts of beauty, a woman ought to know what dress best becomes her. So Castiglione ingeniously remarks that if she perceives herself to be a gay and sprightly beauty, "she ought so to accommodate her gestures, words, and clothes as may all contribute to heighten the charms of it. In the same manner let her who is of a mild and grave temperament by all suitable ways improve what nature has given her. So, likewise, whether she be fatter or leaner than ordinary, or fair or brown, let her use the assistance of dress, but let all art therein be concealed as much as possible; let her appear easy and genteel, without any affectation or taking pains." This again is good advice, and a knowledge of pictures will greatly help a woman to take advantage of it. More especially will the study of painting educate her eye to the appreciation of harmony of colors, of grace of line, of elegance of silhouette, and of dignity of bearing.

A woman whose memory possesses the portraits of Vandyck, Titian, and Bronzino can never consent to be badly dressed, however simple and inexpensive her garments may be. The haunting souvenir of the female figures of Luini, Leonardo, and Botticelli is a sure preservative against awkward gestures, ungraceful bearing, and want of suavity of all kinds. The frequentation of the noble painters of Italy, Flanders, and France is an encouragement to look upon the adornment of beauty not as a matter of vanity, much less as the business of the Tempter, according to the ideas of the ascetics, but rather as a manifestation of culture, a triumph of civilization, like the transformation of the simple eglantine into the resplendent rose.

On the other hand, there are partisans of beauty unadorned. That fascinating but often self-contradictory thinker, Ernest Renan, remarking the total absence of jewels, and even of flowers, in the traditional adornment of the women of his native Brittany, has written a curious page to express his disapproval of the use of ornaments altogether. With antique nudity, this philosopher argues, jewelry had a *raison d'être*, and Greece, taking advantage of certain errors of the East, ventured to cope with that most delicate problem of adorning the masterpiece of nature—a truly beautiful woman. But in our cold climates, and with the current ideas of Christian modesty, jewelry is out of place. What have these ornaments of savages and Bédouines to do with the one and only important thing, namely, the sweetness and innocence of the looks? Can virtue and candor be expressed by jewels? Has there ever been invented a jewel for the eyes? It is true there is the odious henné; but has a woman who respects herself ever used henné? What a horrible idea it is to blacken the golden balustrade of the celestial Jerusalem, and to defile the edges of that sacred fountain in the depths of which we see God and his paradise!

M. Renan goes even further, and protests against color in the service of beauty, maintaining that black and white suffice, because, better than all ornaments, they leave room for dreams of amorous and veiled flesh. But enough of paradoxes. The practice of humanity from time immemorial speaks in favor both of color and adornment, and it is in these conditions that the greatest artists have always represented beauty. So far as concerns the ways of arranging women's hair, no artists have at any time shown themselves so various as the Italian painters of the fifteenth and sixteenth centuries, more especially Piero della Francesca, Sandro Botticelli, Leonardo da Vinci, Titian, Bronzino, and the other great Venetians. Doubtless it may be urged that in those days, when fashion varied not only from one country to another, but from one province and even from one town to another, a painter could never be at a loss for models. It is true that Italian women, like Italian men, enjoyed complete liberty in the arrangement of their hair; there was no one fashion to which all conformed, as is more or less the case in the civilized world of to-day; on the contrary, absolute license reigned in the domain of fashion; but such was the artistic instinct of this favored epoch that taste never had to suffer from excess of liberty. Nevertheless, the coiffures that were invented by the native genius of coquetry, or by the imaginings of rival milliners, were certainly not the only source from which the painters drew inspiration. On the contrary, the painters were themselves the chief professors of the art of coiffure, and the very greatest devoted much attention to the invention of beautiful arrangements and adornments for the hair of their models. Thus Vasari, speaking of Leonardo da Vinci's admirable skill in drawing, mentions with enthusiasm "some heads of women whose coiffures were so graceful and beautiful that Leonardo always imitated them"—coiffures which we may be sure were composed by Leonardo himself, for the drawings in question still exist to charm us by their absolute beauty and complete originality.

One of these drawings at Florence represents the favorite Milanese type which Leonardo has immortalized in his picture of the Virgin and St. Anne, the hair falling in rolling waves, almost in ringlets, over the shoulders, the shorter front locks finely crimped, and brushed forward over the cheeks so as to conceal the ears, a small veil covering the nape, and on the top of the head a flat chignon of coiled braids bound round with a broad band or plaited fillet, over which is a diadem with

HEAD OF A GRACE BY BOTTICELLI

a circular jewel or *ferronnière* in the centre flanked
by small wings, while on each side above the ear
two bunches of frizzed hair escape from beneath
the band, and from the summit of the chignon another bunch of feathery hair rises like a natural
aigrette. In the Museum of Venice another head
by Leonardo is represented with a crown or fillet
of vine branches and leaves, and the hair falling in
ample ringlets on each side of the head below the fillet. In the Ambrosian Library at Milan is a drawing
by Leonardo of a very simple coiffure in which the
hair is parted in the middle; from the front tresses
are taken wherewith to make three triple plaits
or braids, the first one starting on a level with the
eyebrows, the one behind it a little lower, and the
third one a little lower still; then these three braids
are looped up one above the other and tied at the
back of the head, thus holding in position the long
hair that falls in waves behind over the neck.
Other drawings at Vienna, or in the royal collection at Windsor, show exquisite arrangements of
braided hair covered or draped with transparent
veils, and finally at Windsor there is a large
drawing and four sketches of a singular coiffure
which seems to have greatly fascinated Leonardo.
The suggestion evidently came from the head of
the Gorgon Medusa, with horrors armed and curls

FROM A DRAWING BY LEONARDO DA VINCI

of hissing snakes, as Homer has described her in his Odyssey. Leonardo, however, has suppressed the horror, and retained only a strange serpentine arabesque, which forms the *leitmotiv* of this composition of interwoven braids and floating locks,

one of the most fantastic and complicated that the
artist invented, yet not more complicated than
many coiffures that may be seen in the portraits
and pictures of the time.

Beauty and originality of coiffure play a great
rôle in the paintings of Sandro Botticelli (1447–
1510). In his picture of "Calumny," painted from
Lucian's description of a picture by Apelles, doubtless as translated by the artist's friend and adviser
Leone Battista Alberti, a scene of hair-dressing
forms one of the incidents. Alberti's translation
runs thus :

"There is a personage with long ears with two
women, one on each side, namely, Ignorance and
Superstition. Calumny advances in the form of a
beautiful woman, whose face, however, is hardened
by cunning. In her left hand she holds a lighted
torch, and with the other hand she drags along by
the hair a young man who lifts up his hands heav-
enward. Her guide is a pale, hideous man with a
savage face. Two other women, companions of
Calumny, are busied with adorning their mistress ;
these are Treachery and Fraud. Behind them is
Repentance in sordid clothes, followed by Truth,
modest and pure."

The fragment of this great picture reproduced
in our engraving represents the two beautiful

maidens, Treachery and Fraud, dressing the hair of Calumny. Fraud binds her chignon with a ribbon, while Treachery places flowers in her hair. The coiffure of Treachery herself consists of long floating locks, a head-band and veil, and a chignon of braided hair partly enkerchiefed. But perhaps the most beautiful coiffures imagined by Botticelli are those of the three Graces in the picture in the academy at Florence, commonly known as an "Allegory of Spring." The arrangement of the hair of the central figure is peculiarly elegant, consisting entirely of waves and torsades, and one braid passing over the top of the head, the whole without extraneous ornamentation. The figure on the right wears a more elaborate coiffure, with a braided chignon, and two long braids which are wound round the loose switches on each side and joined over the bosom, and attached to a rich brooch or pendant, while the front hair is crimped and frizzed, and carried forward so as to hide the ears entirely, and the loose tresses on the crown entwined with strings of pearls and jewelled pins.

A more richly ornate coiffure is that painted by Botticelli in the beautiful profile portrait now in the Städel Kunst-Institut at Frankfort, representing that great Florentine lady, Lucrezia Tornabuoni, wife of Piero dei Medici, mother of Lorenzo the

TREACHERY AND FRAUD DRESSING THE HAIR OF CALUMNY

Magnificent, and grandmother of Pope Leo X.
The back hair is gathered in a great switch, and
laced with ribbon as far down as the nape, where

WAVES AND TORSADES

it is divided and plaited in two heavy braids ornamented with pearls, which follow the contours of
the corsage, and are knotted on the bosom; another pearl-embroidered braid surrounds the head
vertically, and is coiled into a fantastic chignon;

the line of the parting is marked by a row of pearls, and from it fall three fine braids of different lengths knotted so that the ends hang loose like tassels; these three pendent braids are laced together with strings of small pearls, while on the top of the head is a splendid flower-shaped jewel and an aigrette of peacocks' feathers tilted backward. The strange beauty and fantastic richness of this coiffure of hair and pearls—hair braided, hair waved, hair falling in silky tassels—cannot be described; the picture must be seen in order that the reader may comprehend the supreme taste of the artist, and the magnificent simplicity—if we may so express it—of the arrangement of the hair in such a manner that the form of the head is sedulously respected, and the purity of the silhouette, both of the head and of the neck, always evident beneath the natural veil of golden tresses. This respect of the natural form of the head is a point to which too much attention cannot be paid, for by this sign we recognize the coiffure of the true artist, and by this sign are the inventions of the great painters of the Italian Renaissance distinguished from the monstrous or quaintly voluminous coiffures which the vagaries of fashion, uncontrolled by good taste, have invented in unartistic epochs both before and since. The beauty of the

FROM A FRESCO BY PIERO DELLA FRANCESCA

coiffure which aims purely at bringing into relief
the splendor of the hair, as compared with that in
which the head-dress predominates, is admirably illustrated by the contrast of the two heads by Botticelli with the heads in the accompanying engraving, taken from a fresco by Piero della Francesca, representing Italian ladies of the fifteenth
century wearing the actual coiffures which the
fashion of the hour decreed. The fresco is a grand
work of art, full of character and mystery, but the
coiffures are ephemeral, and at the best merely
curious. On the other hand, the types of feminine
beauty which the artist has portrayed are so striking, the features so pure, and the necks so swanlike,
that we are inclined to believe that the queer cap
worn by one lady is beautiful too, and to be ready
to maintain that the *escoffion* worn by the other is
a marvel of good taste, and the veil thrown over it
a miracle of elegance — so true is it that there are
certain undulating contours, a certain ovalness of
face, a certain fineness in the chiselling of lips, certain droopings of the eyelids, certain bendings of
the head, which ravish us beyond expression, and
hold us fascinated for hours in the contemplation
of portraits of vanished beauty.

VII

VENICE

In the picture by Bronzino (1501–70) reproduced in our engraving the coiffure is simple in arrangement, the hair being merely combed out, braided, and gathered in a net. The net itself, however, was of extreme richness, and in harmony with the magnificent jewelled ornamentation of the corsage, a net of golden threads strung with pearls. Such a costume as this lady wears, all cloth-of-gold, brocaded silk, damask, embroidery, and precious stones, is a monument of a vanished civilization which our modest modern luxury must ever despair of repeating; it is the gown of a lady who lived in a favored land where everything is smiling, and where Nature herself preaches grandeur and magnificence; it is the sumptuous garb of a princess whose life was passed in one of those antique Italian palaces which, gloomy or ruined as they now are, still speak eloquently of the resplendent and superb existence of the Scalas, the Viscontis, the Strozzis, the Gonzagas, the

Medicis, the mighty lords of Verona, Mantua, and Florence. Feminine costume in Italy in the fifteenth and sixteenth centuries harmonized perfectly with the architecture of these palaces, whose colonnades were draped with the precious products of the looms of Venice and the East. Ample and noble in form, it was rich in material and gorgeous in ornamentation. Favored by nature and fortune, Italy was singularly favored by the Muses before and during the early Renaissance, and her women all possessed instinctive good taste. But, above all things, the great artists and the men of letters exercised a sovereign controlling influence over fashion, and preserved it from those wild caprices to which it is exposed when the ladies have no other guide than the vulgar fashion journal. Thus it happens that while the pictures by the oldest Flemish and French masters are, as a rule, merely curious from the point of view of the student of feminine elegance, those of the old Italian masters are full of suggestiveness. A coiffure by Botticelli, or a gown by Ghirlandajo, is as much a touchstone of eternal elegance as the headdress of a Greek statue or the drapery of a Tanagra statuette.

At the same time the Italian literary men devoted much attention to the study of feminine cos-

tume and of the adornment of beauty, and the
poets abound in delicate analyses and notations of
all that is exquisite in the aspect and manners of
women. Firenzuola's *Dialogue on the Beauty of
Women* is a masterpiece of elegant language and
ingenious observation. Lodovico Dolce's Venetian
dialogue, *Della Institutione delle Donne*, is likewise
of extreme interest; and although one cannot rec-
ommend the reading of Alessandro Poccolomini's
book, *La bella Creanza delle Donne*, from the
point of view of edification, yet we should be
sorry not to possess in a discreet corner of our
library this vivacious little manual of feminine elegance in the sixteenth century. As for Castiglione's book on the perfect lady and the perfect
gentleman according to the ideas of the refined
Court of Urbino, we have already intimated the
high esteem in which we hold the author of this
incomparable work. Indeed, how could we not
esteem this noble and cultivated author, without
whose judgment and approbation Raphael and
Buonarotti never thought their works perfect?
How can the Count Baldassar's name ever fade
from the memory of fair women? No writer has
ever spoken more nobly of the social rôle of the
sex, inasmuch as he has made out woman to be
the prime origin of all the arts of civilization in

ELEONORA OF TOLEDO, BY BRONZINO

the following passage, which we beg leave to quote from the Third Book of his *Courtier*.

"Are you not sensible," asks Castiglione, "that whatever exercises are agreeable or taking in the world are so only for the sake of women ? Who would care to dance or to learn all the graceful motions of the body but to please them ? Who has any other end than this in making himself perfect in music ? Who would ever write verses, especially in a vulgar language, but to express the affections raised by women ? Consider what valuable poems, both in Greek and Latin, would the world be deprived of if the poets had no value for that sex ! And, to omit all others, what a loss should we have had if Francis Petrarch, whose love-songs in our language are so divinely fine, had wholly confined himself to Latin, as he certainly would if the love of Laura had not been in the way !"

It is indeed a curious truth that if the love of Laura had not been in the way, as Castiglione quaintly says, Petrarch would have confined himself wholly to Latin, and the modern European languages might have remained undeveloped and non-literary. So Dante, in his *Vita Nuova*, commenting upon one of his own love-sonnets, says : "And, indeed, it is not a great number of years

7

since poetry began to be made in the vulgar
tongue ; the writing of rhymes in spoken language
corresponding to the writing in metre of Latin
verse, by a certain analogy. And I say that it is
but a little while, because if we examine the language of *oco* and the language of *si* (*i.e.*, the languages of Provence and Tuscany) we shall not find
in those tongues any written thing of an earlier
date than the last hundred and fifty years. Also
the reason why certain of a very mean sort obtained at the first some fame as poets is, that before them no man had written verses in the language of *si ;* and of these the first was moved to
the writing of such verses by the wish to make
himself understood of a certain lady unto whom
Latin poetry was difficult."

And the good poets who ventured to write in
the vulgar tongue, wishing to please their lady-
loves, unto whom Latin poetry was difficult, began
at once to sing the charms of fair hair. Thus
Fazio degli Uberti (1326–60), in a canzone so excellent that it has been attributed to Dante, tracing
the portrait of his lady, Angiola of Verona, says:

"I look at the crisp golden-threaded hair
Whereof, to thrall my heart, Love twists a net,
Using at times a string of pearls for bait,
And sometimes with a single rose therein.

"I look at the amorous beautiful mouth,
 The spacious forehead which her locks enclose,
 The small white teeth, the straight and shapely nose,
 And the clear brows of a sweet pencilling.

"I look at her white easy neck, so well
 From shoulders and from bosom lifted out;
 And at her round cleft chin, which beyond doubt
 No fancy in the world could have designed.

"I look at the large arms, so lithe and round,
 At the hands which are white and rosy too,
 At the long fingers, clasped and woven through,
 Bright with the ring which one of them doth wear."*

So Guido Cavalcanti, who was Dante's senior by some fifteen years, in a ballad on a shepherd-maid whom he met one day within a copse, describes her coming

"with waving tresses pale and bright,
 With rosy cheer, and loving eyes of flame,
 Guiding the lambs beneath her wand aright."

Cino da Pistoia (1270–1337), in his lament for Selveggia, cries:

"Ay me, alas! the beautiful bright hair
 That shed reflected gold
 O'er the green growths on either side the way."

* Translation of D. G. Rossetti.

Boccaccio, in his sonnet on his last sight of Fia-
metta, describes how

> " Round her red garland and her golden hair
> I saw a fire about Fiametta's head."

And in another playful sonnet, which, as the trans-
lator, Dante Gabriel Rossetti, has observed, recalls
by the beauty of its color the painted pastorals of
Giorgione, Boccaccio again dwells upon the fascination of golden hair. But this sonnet is so dainty
that we must quote it entirely in Rossetti's ren-
dering :

" OF THREE GIRLS AND OF THEIR TALK

> " By a clear well, within a little field
> Full of green grass and flowers of every hue,
> Sat three young girls, relating (as I knew)
> Their loves. And each had twined a bough to shield
> Her lovely face ; and the green leaves did yield
> The golden hair their shadow ; while the two
> Sweet colors mingled, both blown lightly through
> With a soft wind forever stirr'd and still'd.
> After a little while one of them said
> (I heard her) : ' Think ! If ere the next hour struck
> Each of our lovers should come here to-day,
> Think you that we should fly or feel afraid ?'
> To whom the others answered : ' From such luck
> A girl would be a fool to run away.' "

As for Petrarch, he will hear of none but golden
locks. His Laura has black eyes and a beautiful
white face, and in the second canzone he declares

VIOLANTE, BY PALMA VECCHIO

that "never was golden hair twisted into a blond braid by a lady so beautiful as she who has deprived me of all freedom of will." Elsewhere he says, "The blond-hair neighbor of the eyes that lead my years to so speedy an end, eclipses the brilliancy of gold, and of topazes on snow in the sunshine." And, again, he speaks of "the golden tresses that ought to fill the sun with boundless jealousy"; and elsewhere, "in the golden hair of Laura, Love has hidden the bonds with which he grasps me"; and again: "Her head was like fine gold, her face white as snow, her eyelashes were black as ebony, and her eyes were two stars; therefore Love did not stretch his bow in vain.". . . "The suave breeze unfolds and tosses the gold that Love has spun and woven with his hand; by the beautiful eyes of Laura and by her tresses he enthralls my weary heart.". . . "The forehead and the hair so beautiful that, to see them in summer at noonday, they surpass the sun in brilliancy.". . . "The eyes of which I have spoken so warmly, and the arms and the hands and the feet and the face that ravished me and made me something distinct from all other men, the crimped hair shining like pure gold, and the flash of angelic laughter that made for me an earthly paradise, are now a little dust." Then, finally, when Laura appears to Petrarch for the last time in a dream, the poet exclaims, with the obstinacy of eternal admiration, " Are these the blond tresses and the golden braids that hold me still in bondage, and are these the eyes that were my sun ?"

Such being the unanimity of the poets of the day, golden hair became necessarily fashionable. There was no alternative, the more so as the testimony of the ancients was also found to be in favor of blond locks. From Homer to Apuleius the admiration of fair hair persists. Aphrodite was a blonde, so was the beautiful Byrrhene and the soubrette Photis, whose charms Apuleius has daintily described in a passage which everybody knows, but which, doubtless, few remember. Blond, too, was Milton's Eve, who

"as a veil down to the slender waist
Her unadorned golden tresses wore
Dishevel'd, but in wanton ringlets waved
As the vine curls her tendrils."

Therefore Firenzuola, in his description of the beauty of the ideal woman of the epoch of the Renaissance in Italy, requires her to have beautiful hair, fine, soft, and blond, either the color of gold or of honey, or like the bright rays of the resplendent sun. This blond hair must be crisp,

abundant, and long, as we see it in the coiffures
of Botticelli's figures, and especially in the portraits by the Venetian painter Palma Vecchio
(1480–1548), who delights to depict his beautiful
daughter Violante with her luxuriant hair hanging in long and voluminous tresses, adorned with a
simple fillet of ribbon, or with a string of pearls
and a jewel over the forehead. This same figure of Violante appears constantly in the pictures
of Titian, for whom she frequently posed, and
who, like Palma, delights in golden hair. Titian,
however, generally paints a composed coiffure, discreetly adorned with strings of pearls and a jewel
or two, rather than loose flowing tresses. But
both Titian and Palma, and all the Venetians of
the early Renaissance, paint blond hair; Botticelli's women, too, are all blondes; and yet blond
hair was the exception in Italy. Evidently the
Italian ladies of the fifteenth and sixteenth centuries corrected nature, as the Cynthias, the Lydias,
and the Lalages did in the days of Ovid, Martial,
and Juvenal. The transformation of the natural
brunette into the artificial blonde was obtained by
means of dyes and bleaching lotions. If the truth
were known, it would perhaps be discovered that
Petrarch's Laura dyed her hair just as Poppæa
dyed hers at the request of Nero, and doubtless by

the same means, for in the Roman writers we read about processes of bleaching the hair and drying it in the sun exactly similar to those mentioned by the Venetian authors, and illustrated by Vecellio in his book of costumes. The shades affected by the Roman ladies were also the same as those that were fashionable in Renaissance Italy. There was the brilliant blond, or *rutilus*, the golden or tawny blond, and the blond *cendré*, as the French call it, or, as Firenzuola's terms run, golden blond, honey blond, and *lionato* or tawny.

Thus we read in that strangely enigmatical treatise of love and architecture the *Hypnerotomachia*, written in the middle of the fifteenth century by the Venetian monk Francesco Colonna, the description which Polia gives of the beginning of Poliphilo's invincible passion. "I was sitting," she says, "according to the custom of beautiful young girls, at the window, or rather on the balcony, of my palace. My blond hair—my blond hair, the delight of young girls — was floating loosely over my snowy shoulders. Bathed with an ambrosia destined to render it as brilliant as threads of gold, it was drying in the rays of ardent Phœbus. Proud to serve me, a maid was combing my hair with infinite care. No, I dare to say the hair of Andromeda did not seem as beautiful to Perseus, nor

PEARLS AND JEWELS, FROM A PICTURE BY TITIAN

that of Photis to Lucius. Suddenly Poliphilo, having caught sight of me, could not remove from me his burning and devouring looks, and from that moment a ray of the sun of love was kindled within his bosom."

Such is the first testimony that we have in Italian literature of the existence of that "arte biondeggiante" which became a craze and a scandal in the fifteenth and sixteenth centuries, and which has survived even to the present day. Thanks to this art, of which far be it from us to speak evil, the genius of woman is enabled to create that rare and delicious combination of fair hair and dark eyes of which unassisted nature is so niggardly. Thanks to the "arte biondeggiante," the modern world is full of beauties like the chorus of virgins that Joachim du Bellay celebrates in his epithalamium of Marguerite of France, Duchess of Savoy:

> "Leurs tresses blondoyantes
> Voletoient ondoyantes
>   Sur leur col blanchissant ;
> Leurs yeux comme planètes,
> Sur leurs faces brunettes
>   Alloient resplendissant."

VIII

THE SPANISH TOQUE

ALMOST all those who have written dainty treatises about the beauty and adornment of women
have referred to the opinion of Apuleius as regards
the question of hair. It is even allowable to imagine
that the austere Tertullian, when he thundered so eloquently against the use of hair-dye and wigs and
fantastic wimples, had not forgotten the passage of
the *Golden Ass* in which is related the amorous ad-
venture of Lucius and Photis. For Tertullian, it
must be remembered, the son of a centurion of the
Proconsul of Africa, born at Carthage about the
year A.D. 160, always lived in his native town, where
he practised law before he became the champion of
Christianity. His boyhood and youth coincided
with the epoch of the oratorical triumphs of Apuleius. Many a time he must have been among the
enthusiastic listeners who applauded the lectures
and readings of the great rhetorician in the theatre
of Carthage, and who marvelled at his novel prose,
so rich in color, so impressionistic, so crisp and pictur-

esque, so widely different from the classical prose of Rome. At any rate, the prose of Apuleius is the model which Tertullian followed in his own literary efforts. This mode of expression thus came to prevail in the church of Carthage; and through the church of Carthage, which played a preponderating rôle in the history of Western Christianity, the picturesque style was transmitted to Spain and the other European communities, and so presided over the birth of modern literature. Thus the true literary ancestor of the Latin Church may be said to be Apuleius, the author of that more than piquant *Golden Ass*, in which we read the following panegyric of hair:

"If you cut off the hair of the most beautiful of women and deprive her face of its natural ornament, nay, were she of heavenly descent, engendered of the sea, nurtured in the midst of the waves, in a word, Venus herself, accompanied by the Loves and Graces, adorned with her girdle and perfumed with the sweetest odors, if her head were bald she could not please even her own Vulcan.

"What is there more charming than hair of a beautiful color, neatly arranged, shining softly or brilliantly in the sun? Some hair is of blond more resplendent than the sun, but darker towards the roots. Other hair, black as the plumage of a crow, plays changefully in the light like the breast of a pigeon, and, perfumed with the essences of Araby, combed out and braided behind, resembles a mirror which embellishes and reflects in the eye of the lover the image of her whom he adores. Is it not charming, again, to see a great quantity of hair, artistically arranged on the top of the head, or else, when the hair is of exceptional length, loose and floating over the shoulders? In short, there is something so distinguished in beautiful hair that even though a woman should appear with all sorts of ornaments and robes covered with gold and precious stones, her efforts are in vain unless she have withal fine hair."

Blacker and more brilliant than jet must be the hair of the Persian beauty; and as for the length, we must hear Firdousi describe the charms of the heroic Roudabah, daughter of Mehrab, King of Cabul, whose black tresses were so abundant and so long that one day from the top of a tower of the royal castle where she was taking the air, having perceived Zal riding back from the chase, she let them fall slowly to the foot of the tower in order to help him to climb the wall, for her heart had suddenly leaped within her bosom at the sight of the unknown lord, and Zal used the solid coils of these strong and magnificent ringlets like the rungs of a

MARGUERITE OF PARMA, BY COELLO

ladder to climb up and approach the intrepid re-
cluse.

In the annals of Moorish Spain we might dis-
cover romantic stories that would be a match for
this one. In the art of Spain, however, we do not
find much that is suggestive in the way of coiffure.
Certainly the blue-black tresses of the Madonnas of
Murillo are beautiful; admirable, too, are the combs
and patillas and the mantos of the coiffure of the
various provinces of Spain, but their interest is
local, for none but Spanish women can wear them.
As for the court coiffures, the court costumes, and
the court ladies immediately after the grand epoch
of Philip IV. and of Velasquez, we have only to
read Madame d'Aulnoy's *Mémoires de la Cour d'Es-
pagne* in order to confirm us in the unfavorable
opinion which the portraits of the time have given
us. Of the court ladies, Madame d'Aulnoy says:
" They are almost all short, and extremely thin and
slender; their skin is soft, black, and painted; their
features regular, their eyes full of fire, their hair
black and abundant, their hands pretty, and their
feet of surprising smallness. Their dress becomes
them so ill that unless one is accustomed to it one
finds it unendurable." And elsewhere the same
observer, speaking of the queen, Louise d'Orléans,
niece of Louis XIV., who married Charles II., son

of Philip IV., writes: "The queen could not help smiling when she saw herself for the first time dressed in the Spanish fashion, for, with the exception of her alone, I never saw any foreigner who looked well in this costume. After passing through several rooms which are truly admirable, I found her in a cabinet, painted and gilded and filled with large looking-glasses fixed in the wood-work of the walls. She was seated on an ottoman near the window, and making some embroidery of gold lace and blue silk. Her hair was parted in the middle, and arranged in a braid laced with big pearls and attached to her girdle; she wore a rose velvet gown embroidered with silver, and ear-rings that hung down over her bosom, and so heavy that she took one of them off so that I might feel the weight, which astonished me."

The court coiffures during the preceding reign of Philip IV. may be seen in the pictures of Velasquez, in the faded blond hair of the infantas, parted on one side, and looped in a bang over the forehead, or parted in the middle, prodigiously frizzled, and tied at the ends with ribbons and jewels in a manner that refined taste can scarcely approve.

The finest examples of costume and coiffure that Spanish art affords are to be found in the portraits by the Portuguese artist Alonso Coello (1505 – 90), a pupil of Raphael and of Antonio Moro, and court painter to Philip II. of Spain. Our illustrations reproduce two exquisite works by Coello. One is the portrait of Marguerite of Parma, and the other is the portrait of Maria of Austria, daughters of Charles V., Emperor of Germany and King of Spain, the first of the name. Both these pictures are in the Brussels Museum. Thus, after all, the models in question were not Spaniards, but Austrians, and the painter was not a Spaniard, but a Portuguese; nor is there anything particularly Spanish about either of the portraits except the head-dress worn by Marguerite of Parma, which is generally known as a Spanish toque — a fashion which afterwards gained great favor at the court of France, and remains an example always worthy of imitation. The wavy hair is brushed back from the forehead and up from the neck, and gathered somewhat loosely in a high chignon surmounted by a velvet toque, with a bouquet of feathers on the left, the toque being richly ornamented with jewelry in the form of mounted pearls and chains laced diagonally. The hair, too, is adorned with pearls and jewels, among which is a serpent of enamelled gold. Around her neck, below the not yet too voluminous ruffle, the princess wears a magnificent collar of mounted jewels, and the general aspect of the lady and of her attire is noble, sumptuous, and in good taste, consideration, of course, being made of the conditions in which she lived. Evidently so rich a costume and so resplendent a coiffure as this could scarcely be worn by young ladies who play lawn-tennis, ride on the top of mail-coaches, chatter like magpies, and are generally unquiet in their movements and gestures. A dignified costume requires a dignified wearer. However, it must be stated that the costume reproduced in our engraving is one that was worn by Marguerite of Parma for riding on horseback, and Brantôme tells us that the black velvet Spanish toque, either simple or trimmed with feathers and jewels, was the coiffure considered by his fair contemporaries to be most becoming for riding as well as for evening dress. For wearing a Spanish toque the hair may be simply curled in front, and held behind in a net or *crépine* of silk or gold thread. The form of the toque may also be varied by the greater or less elevation of the crown, and by the addition of a brim, either circular or of irregular shape, and adorned with a jewelled band and an aigrette, such as we see in the portraits of Marie Stuart when she first appeared at the court of France in all the brilliancy of her youth and beauty. The coquette, too, will put new expression into the Spanish toque by

MARIA OF AUSTRIA, BY COELLO

wearing it a little on one side, thus adding piquancy to grace.

A more elaborate and curious coiffure is that worn by Maria of Austria in the engraved portrait given. The hair, parted in the middle, is brushed off the forehead, braided and coiled in a chignon behind, while on the top of the head is a little frizzed toupet, and on the left side a bunch of small curls and a tassel of crimped hair, the curls arranged star-wise, with a jewel and pendant in the centre; a diadem of gold set with precious stones has a large jewel and pendant in the middle, falling just over the parting; and the coiffure is completed by a fine white gauze veil or scarf edged with lace, to each point of which is attached a spangle. This scarf is tied in the middle of the corsage to a ring from which hangs a jewelled cross with three pear-shaped pearls suspended from it. Round the waist is a heavy jewelled girdle, and the skirt is fastened down the front by means of jewelled clasps, while the upper hem of the corsage is trimmed with a band of jewels. The high collar is enriched with spangles, and terminates in a dainty frill closely enframing the face, and the tags that adorn the ample velvet sleeves are beautifully wrought with gold and crystal. Notice also the slashed gloves with the finger-rings showing through the *crevés,* the taper fingers of the white ungloved hand, the ear-droppers fixed in the doubly pierced ears by double rings. Truly this is a most noble lady and a most brave costume.

In these two portraits of the daughters of Charles V. we see excellent specimens of the taste of the sixteenth century in jewelry. The fashion of the day, more especially in France and in the Low Countries, was to adorn the hair with a profusion of *enseignes, agrafes,* and *ballaux,* as the old French terms are, the latter meaning balls of gold or silver adorned with precious stones and mounted on pins, which were stuck in the hair. *Agrafes* are merely buckles or clasps like the serpent worn by Marguerite of Parma. *Enseignes* are those big jewels such as we see fixed in the hair of both these ladies, and such as we find described in great numbers in the inventory of Gabrielle d'Estrées, composed of diamonds, rubies, sapphires, and pendent pearls, set in elaborate gold mounts enriched with colored enamels—jewels of remarkable design due to the happy alliance of Flemish skill and Italian taste, and designed by the great artists of the Renaissance, Benvenuto Cellini, Androuet du Cerceau, Théodore de Bry, and Pierre Woeriot—the latter a famous designer of rings.

IX

THE EIGHTEENTH CENTURY

" When one writes about women," said Diderot, "one should dip the pen in the rainbow and dry the lines with the dust of butterflies' wings. It suffices not to talk about women, and to talk well, Monsieur Thomas ; you must make me see them. Place them before my eyes like so many thermometers of the smallest vicissitudes of manners and usages."

If we were to follow Diderot's advice in speaking of the coiffures that were successively *à la mode* in Europe during the seventeenth and eighteenth centuries, and if we were to avail ourselves even sparingly of the documents afforded by the painting and the sculpture of that epoch, we should have to write a large volume instead of a short chapter, for the arrangement of hair was never more capricious than it was in the reigns of Louis XIV., Louis XV., and Louis XVI., when France became definitively the Queen of Fashion for the whole modern world. Therefore

Mr. Addison, in the ninety-eighth *Spectator* (June 22, 1711), maintained that a lady's head-dress is the most variable thing in all nature. "Within my own memory," he wrote, "I have seen it rise and fall above thirty degrees. About ten years ago it shot up to a very great height, insomuch that the female part of our species were much taller than the men. The women were of such enormous stature that we appeared as grasshoppers before them. For my own part, as I do not love to be insulted by women who are taller than myself, I admire the sex much more in their present humiliation, which has reduced them to their natural dimensions, than when they had extended their persons and lengthened themselves out into formidable and gigantic figures. I am not for adding to the beautiful edifices of Nature, nor for raising any whimsical superstructure upon her plans. I must therefore repeat it, that I am highly pleased with the coiffure now in fashion, and think it shews the good sense which at present very much reigns among the valuable part of the sex."

Further on in the same essay Mr. Spectator gives the following excellent advice about dressing hair: "I would desire the fair sex to consider how impossible it is for them to add anything that can be

ornamental to what is already the masterpiece of
Nature. The head has the most beautiful appearance, as well as the highest station in a human
figure. Nature has laid out all her art in beautify-
ing the face; she has touched it with vermilion,
planted in it a double row of ivory, made it the
seat of smiles and blushes, lighted it up and en-
livened it with the brightness of the eyes, hung it
on each side with curious organs of sense, given it
airs and graces that cannot be described, and surrounded it with such a flowing shade of hair as
sets all its beauties in the most agreeable light. In
short, she seems to have designed the head as the
cupola to the most glorious of her works; and
when we load it with such a pile of supernumerary
ornaments we destroy the symmetry of the human
figure, and foolishly contrive to call off the eye
from great and real beauties to childish gewgaws,
ribbands, and bone-lace."

While not entirely agreeing with Mr. Addison in
his sweeping condemnation of gewgaws and ribbons, we think that the most tasteful and refined
coiffures are those in which the predominant ele-
ment is the natural hair and not the gewgaw. The
basis of fashion in coiffure is the hair, and in dress
it is the garment; and as the component parts of
dress are continually changing from great to little,

from long to short, from tight to loose, and *vice versa*, so the coiffure of women has continually varied from close to floating, from flat to fluffy, from compact to voluminous, from absence of ornament to excess of ornament. At one time the head-dress grows in height, and when the maximum of verticality has been obtained, the direction of obliquity is gradually substituted for it, as in the *hennins*, or steeple coiffures; and then horizontality takes the place both of verticality and of obliquity, and in the *escoffion* the coiffure grows out laterally in the form of enormous cushions. All these growths of coiffure, being more or less architectural and requiring important frame-works and accessories, invite ornament, and the natural tendency of ornament being to creep, encroach, and monopolize, the hair little by little disappears, and the gewgaws and ribbons remain triumphant. Then comes the inevitable reaction, and under some sociological or private influence the gewgaw is banished, the natural hair restored to favor, and the whole process from simplicity to complexity begins over again.

Since the end of the Middle Ages the coiffure of modern Europe has been influenced by three series of phenomena, among which must be mentioned first of all the artistic movement of the Renais-

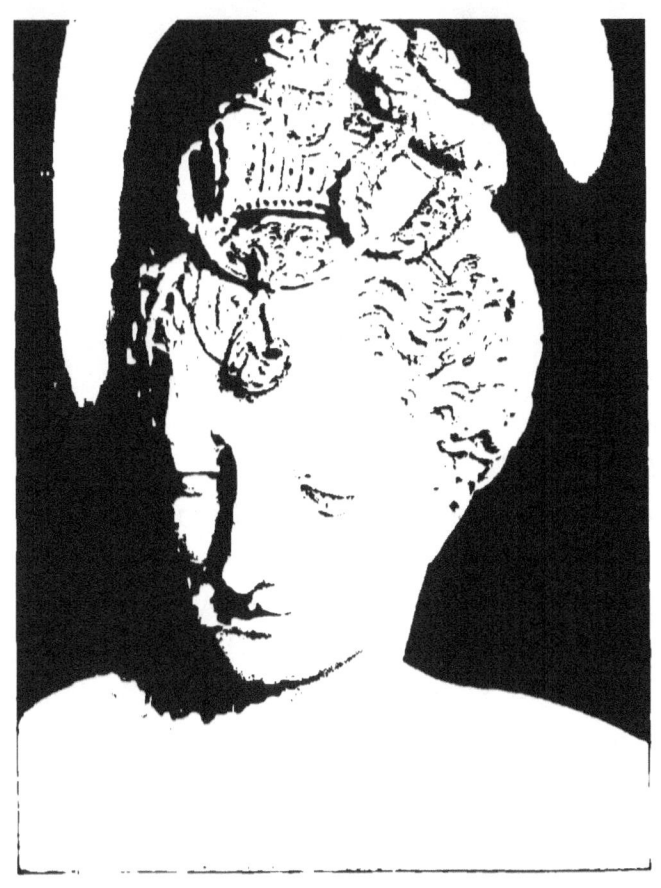

DIANE DE POITIERS, BY JEAN GOUJON

sance, which called attention to the models of classical antiquity and created new models of its own,
such as we find in the portraits of the great Italian
artists, and in the work of the French artists of the

sixteenth century, like Jean Goujon (1515–72), Jean Cousin (1501–90), Germain Pilon (1515–90), and Barthélemy Prieur (died 1611), who adapted the severe and dignified style of antique form and ornament to the requirements of the voluptuous court of Henry II., sacrificing somewhat of nobleness, it is true, but superadding a grace and elegance that are purely French. Examples of the ideal of feminine beauty thus obtained may be found in the museum of the Louvre in the admirable figures by Germain Pilon forming a group of three destined to support the shrine of Ste.-Geneviève, and in Jean Goujon's famous figure of Poitiers represented as the Huntress Diana, with a coiffure of admirable complexity and gracefulness of form. These coiffures, like the finest which Italian, Roman, and Hellenic art afford in the epochs of most refined culture, owe their beauty to the arrangement of the hair, and to the general silhouette rather than to the ornamentation. We might even go so far as to say that these coiffures are well and firmly drawn, remembering that the art of dressing hair is really a humble branch of sculpture, and that, as Sir Joshua Reynolds says in his *Discourses*, though it is difficult to define what grace is, we feel that its natural foundation is correctness of design. The moment that the beauty of classical antiquity was

revealed, whether at Rome, Florence, Fontaine-
bleau, or Nuremberg, the moment the art of the
Renaissance became triumphant, the fantastic coiffures of the Middle Ages, conceived without regard
to the form of the head and without respect to
the proportions of the human body and its various
parts, were inevitably condemned, and the only
traces of them to be found nowadays are in remote
survivals observable in the costumes of religious
orders, and in the quaint caps and head-dresses
that are worn by the country people in France,
Germany, Holland, and Hungary.

The second series of phenomena is connected
with the Reformation and the concomitant movement in favor of asceticism, which naturally caused
women to do away with gewgaws and ribbons,
and to dress their hair with all simplicity. Naturally, from the point of view of artistic beauty,
little good can be expected of asceticism, while
Protestantism is obviously a cold and unprofitable
nursery-ground for feminine elegance. Nevertheless, there is one kind of coiffure not without
charm which, we might almost say, is peculiarly
characteristic of Protestant countries, inasmuch as
it prevailed for two and a half centuries in the
Netherlands and in England, and has not yet entirely disappeared in the latter country. This is

the coiffure of Mlle. La Vallière, the hair parted in the middle and brushed flat on the top of the head, with bunches of ringlets on each side and a chignon behind. The quantity of the side ringlets varies, and also their length ; sometimes we find a large bouquet of ringlets, and at other times only two or three long ringlets, very precisely curled. Furthermore, as coquetry is stronger even than Protestantism, a small quantity of ornament was gradually added in the shape of long ear-droppers, and a slender diadem with light pendants attached on each side, as we see in the accompanying engraving representing a group of Dutch ladies walking, from a picture by David Teniers (1610–85).

The third series of phenomena begins with the glorious reign of Louis XIV., and the supremacy and universal initiative which France henceforward assumed in European civilization. When Louis XIV. came to the throne the table was clear. The universe was once more mere malleable clay which the future Grand Monarque was destined to model after his own magnificent ideas. His radiant Majesty was passionately in love with the niece of his minister, Cardinal Mazarin, the beautiful Marie Mancini, *cette créature splendidement charpentée*, as Saint-Evremond calls her, whose portrait by

DUTCH LADIES WALKING, FROM A PAINTING BY DAVID TENIERS

Pierre Mignard (1610–95) now hangs in the Berlin Museum, resplendent with youth and vivacity, her rich wavy hair massed around her face entirely without ornament. From this simple coiffure *en cheveux* were developed in a few scores of years all the monstrous arrangements which provoked the sagacious criticism of Mr. Addison, and which we shall carefully abstain from mentioning, inasmuch as our design is neither to write a history of coiffure nor to classify its archæology, but merely to call attention to certain examples which seem to us to retain permanent suggestiveness and durable charm—examples which we shall find in the reigns of Louis XV. and Louis XVI. rather than in that of " Le Roi Soleil."

We cannot speak of the material beauty of the Frenchwoman of the eighteenth century without mentioning the exhaustive and masterly studies of Edmond and Jules de Goncourt, *La Femme au XVIIième Siècle*, and *L'Art du XVIIième Siècle*. All who wish to comprehend the modifications of French physiognomy in the interval between Le Brun and Latour must consult the great mass of literary, historical, and artistic documents which these authors have so admirably co-ordinated. In their volumes may be seen the transition from the pagan serenity and superb repose of the princesses

of the reign of Louis XIV. in their mythological
surroundings to the most piquant, delicate, and ex-
pressive beauties of the Regency and the reign of
Louis XV. The women of the reign of Louis XIV.
are bovine, Junonian, fleshly, and material. The
women of the reign of Louis XV. are refined, ani-
mated, slender; their faces are illumined with intelligence; their mouths are mobile with irony;
their eyes shine with the fever of pleasure; their
physiognomy seems to be impressed with all the
qualities of the comedies of Marivaux, the grace,
the taste, the coquetry, and withal the tender and
loving heart of Sylvia and Araminthe. These ladies rouged their cheeks, but they required a rouge
"*qui dise quelque chose.*" The rouge worn by a
lady of quality was different from that worn by the
court lady, by the *bourgeoise*, or by the actress; it
was a mere tinge, a simple *soupçon*, an impercep-
tible touch. As some cruel wit put it:

> "Cette artificieuse rougeur
> Qui supplée au défaut de celle
> Que jadis causait la pudeur."

Then, besides the *nuance* of rouge, the toilet of
the face needed to be completed by patches, by
those little pieces of black sticking-plaster which
the poets called "*des mouches dans le lait*"—those

MARIE MANCINI, BY PIERRE MIGNARD

mouches that were cut in the forms of hearts, crescents, moons, stars, and comets, and hung out as love-baits, each with its special name — *l'assassine* at the corner of the eye, *la majesteuse* on the forehead, *l'enjouée* in the laughing dimple, *la galante* in the middle of the cheek, and *la friponne* near the lips. Finally must be mentioned the fashion of powdered hair, which, undesirable as it is, nevertheless lends a particular piquancy to sparkling eyes and youthful faces.

Towards the end of the eighteenth century fashion changes entirely, and the kind of grace desired is no longer piquant, but touching and sentimental, and the women proceed to compose their faces according to the new ideal painted by Greuze and described by Jean Jacques Rousseau. The favorite type is characterized by ingenuousness, candor, languishing tenderness; it is at once virginal and rustic, and its garments are veils of whiteness and gauzes of simplicity.

Meanwhile the coiffeur, the Parisian dress-maker, the " Poupée de la Rue Saint-Honoré," and finally the fashion journal, came into glorious existence, and all Europe was guided by the modes of Paris, and tributary to the art, the commerce, and the industry of the French capital—thanks, as *La Galerie des Modes* says, not to mere caprice, " but to the in-

ventive genius of the French ladies in all that concerns dress, and, above all, to the fine and delicate
taste which characterizes the smallest trifles made
by their hands." The "Poupée de la Rue Saint-
Honoré" was the predecessor of the modern fashion journal, being a life-size doll which was dressed,
undressed, and redressed in the latest taste of Ver-
sailles or the Palais Royal, while replicas were sent
to England, Germany, Italy, and Spain, until the
day when towards the middle of the century some
ingenious persons conceived the idea of illustrated
fashion journals, and announced in their prospec-
tuses that henceforward, through their efforts, for-
eigners would no longer be obliged to trust to dolls,
"which are always imperfect, and very dear, while
at the best they can give but a vague idea of our
fashions."

It is not our purpose to speak of the prodigious
mobility of French fashions in dress during the
eighteenth century; let it suffice to say that the
changes followed very closely the various sentimental transformations of the physiognomy of
the woman of the day, accompanied her beauty,
suited themselves to her tastes, and composed for
her charms an appropriate frame or setting of
stuffs, colors, and forms. Nowadays these variations which were successively proclaimed indispen-

STUDY OF A HEAD, BY WATTEAU

sable by the decrees of the fashion of the day have
become indifferent to us; the inevitable process of
elimination has thrown aside all that was merely
ephemeral and without style; and thus, at the
present day, when we examine the paintings and
engravings of the eighteenth century, previous to
the Revolution, we remark in a general way three
leading types—that invented by the painter Watteau, the Louis XV. type with paniers and a low
coiffure, and the Louis XVI. type with the high
coiffure familiar to us through the portraits of
Marie Antoinette. Of these types the noblest is
that which Watteau invented by means of his
own exquisite genius, and of certain elements
borrowed from the Venetians and the personages
of the Italian Comedy — the ample robe starting
from the neck, plaited in the back like an abbé's
cloak, and floating loosely down to the feet, the
arms emerging flowerlike from short sleeves filled
with *engageantes* of lace. With this robe Watteau imagined a coiffure which, after the example
of Leonardo da Vinci, he studied in scores of
sketches in *sanguine* that form the delight of delicate eyes. No painter has drawn more amorously
than Watteau the voluptuous contours of hair
brushed up from the nape of the neck and back
from the brow, and coiled in the form of a per-

fumed helmet on the crown, or twisted into a simple chignon tied round with a fillet. No painter has rendered more delicately than Watteau the charm of the movements of a woman's head and neck; the fascination of blond flesh, white and silky like the petal of a camellia, the delight of flavescent hair, ruddy like the golden tints of sunset, and forming a luminous nimbus around the head; the transition from the warm tones of the hair to the mat sheenless white of the neck formed by the short downy hair, the *cheveux follets* that curl over the nape, and seem spangled by the light; the rare beauty of the short soft hair that curls naturally behind the ears. The type of feminine beauty, seen and materialized by Watteau, is one of the truly great and precious inventions of art, as great, as original, as fascinating as the types of beauty which we owe to Botticelli, Leonardo, Luini, and Raphael.

Beside Watteau's figures all the other feminine types of the eighteenth century appear dull and pretentious, though some of the high coiffures, it must be admitted, were wonderful works of extravagant art. An excellent and comparatively tasteful specimen of one of these coiffures is given in the bust reproduced in our illustration, being the portrait of the sister of Louis XVI.,

BUST OF MARIE ADÉLAÏDE

Marie Adélaïde, Queen of Sardinia (1759–1802). This coiffure is an architectural monument in hair, the work of one of those masculine capillary artists who first made their appearance in modern Europe in the eighteenth century, and of whom the most famous were Legros, Frédéric, and Léonard, who, mounted on a ladder, as the satirists of the day used to say :

"Bâtissait des cheveux le galant édifice."

The great revolutionist in coiffure was Legros, who was cook to the Comte de Bellemare before he opened an academy, composed of three classes, in which he taught valets de chambre, chambermaids, and coiffeuses the new art of hair-dressing based upon the proportions of the head and the character of the face, *la proportion de la tête et l'air du visage*, and upon the principles and precepts laid down by the artist in the year 1765 in his great and amusing work, *Art de la Coiffure des Dames Françaises*, which was the starting-point of a complete philosophy of the toilet, and of the most extravagant vagaries in head-gear that the world has ever seen, even more various than the three hundred coiffures of the wife of Marcus Aurelius. Before the end of the century did not Paris see ladies wearing on their heads coiffures *à l'inoculation*, where the triumph of vaccination was allegorized by means of a serpent, a club, a rising sun, and an olive-tree covered with fruit? And the coiffure *à la belle Poule*, which was adorned with a frigate in full sail? And the coiffure *au Parc anglais*, where the hair was made the foundation on which were figured landscapes with meadows, trees, running brooks, and browsing sheep? And the coiffure *à la Monte au ciel*, which inspired the English and French caricaturists with such pleasant inventions? All these wild conceits will be found minutely depicted in the prints of the last century, and carefully classified in the portfolios of the Bibliothèque Nationale at Paris. There we will leave them to the solicitude of the curious and the vain researches of frivolous archæologists, for it is not our desire to weary our fair readers with a multitude of vain details, and so cause them to wrinkle their foreheads with a frown of dissatisfaction. We prefer to leave to ruthless Time that ungrateful task—as Shakespeare hath it in his incomparable sonnets—which

> ". . . doth transfix the flourish set on youth
> And delves the parallels in beauty's brow."
> (Sonnet LX.)

BUST OF MARIE ADÉLAÏDE—REVERSE VIEW

X

THE ROMANTIC PERIOD

ABOUT the year 1780 the reaction against the extravagant coiffures to which we have already referred set in, under the influence of the writings of Jean Jacques Rousseau. The dresses were *à la turque, à la créole, à l'anglaise,* and, before the Revolution broke out, the Parisian ladies, in their thirst for simplicity, had reached a point where they found nothing simple enough unless it was *à l'enfant.* During the Revolution fashion became entirely emancipated, and, in the state of anarchy which ensued, Madame Tallien reigned, but did not govern; her influence, however, contributed perhaps to popularize the return to Greek and Roman models, which the discovery of Pompeii and Herculaneum had once more brought into notice, and which the great painter David adapted to the modern spirit in his popular compositions. The Directory continued the movement in favor of *anticomanie,* and added to it *anglomanie,* and the craze for new inventions once more possessed the

Parisian ladies, their milliners, and their coiffeurs. Hence the invention of innumerable wigs, *à l'an-glaise, à l'espagnole, à la Venus, à la Titus, à la Caracalla, à l'Aspasie, à la Sapho.* One day nets were in fashion, the next day chignons, and the next the golden spirals of long ringlets. Aigrettes, feathers, plates and diadems of gold, triple chains of gold, strings of pearls, the *corymbion* and the *capillaments* of the Roman empresses were successively added to the arsenal of accessories with which the coquettes adorned their hair, and Madame Tallien appeared at a ball at the Opéra with rings on her toes and her bosom covered with diamonds, while Madame Récamier persisted in the simplicity of her virginal white robes and her coiffure of short curls bound by a simple fillet—Madame Récamier, whose beauty has become legendary and typical, thanks to her romantic life, and above all perhaps to the portrait, now in the Louvre, by which David has immortalized her features. Of this epoch we shall care to remember, perhaps, only one coiffure, somewhat in the style of that worn by Madame Récamier, somewhat Greek, too, in its simplicity, and yet peculiarly characteristic of many of the best and most interesting portraits of the second half of the eighteenth century. This is the arrangement of loose curls bound by a mod-

erately broad ribbon shown in our engraving of
the portrait of the beautiful Countess of Albany,
by the French painter François Xavier Fabre
(1766–1837), of Montpellier. This portrait is hung
in the Uffizi Gallery, at Florence, side by side with
a portrait of Alfieri, by the same artist, and no one
can look at it without feeling attracted and interested by the personality of the model, whose name
is inseparably linked with that of the great Italian
poet. Married to the pretender Charles Stuart,
the Countess of Albany took refuge in a convent
in order to escape from the brutality of her drunk-
en husband, after whose death she retired to Florence, where she died in 1824, at the age of seventy-
two. Alfieri, who became deeply attached to her,
has celebrated her name and her misfortunes in his
works and in a special biography. She was the
golden chain that held captive the poet's fickle
heart; without her, he says, he would have produced nothing of any worth — *senza laquella non
avrei fatto nullo di buono.* The remains of Alfieri
and of the Countess of Albany are buried together
in a common tomb in the church of Santa Croce,
at Florence, between the tomb of Michael Angelo
and that of Machiavelli.

With the portrait of the Empress Josephine by
Prud'hon (1758–1823), and of the Countess Re-

gnault de Saint-Jean d'Angély, by the Baron Gérard (1770–1836), we come to the palmy days of the Empire and the splendor of the court of Napoleon I. Prud'hon, who possessed the spirit of ancient Greece, whereas David possessed only the letter, painted Josephine in the fresh background of the park of La Malmaison, her hair bound in the antique style by a triple jewelled fillet, smiling, somewhat sentimental, too gentle a creature for such a mighty husband. Gérard has painted the Countess Regnault with simple waved *bandeaux* covering the ears and two little pendent ringlets—a coiffure that has a suggestion of classical antiquity for those who are familiar with the busts of the imperial families of the Roman Empire, and a coiffure which, whether loosely undulated or smoothly brushed, will always please those who, like Sir Joshua Reynolds, would always have the hair "so braided as to ascertain the size and shape of the head." The costume of the Countess is altogether in antique style, and the shoulders and bosom are covered merely with transparent tulle, the beautiful arms being left bare. The two coiffures here represented seem to us worthy of admiration and characteristic of the epoch, though of course at the imperial court the hair of the ladies was dressed with much more splendor, especially on ceremo-

THE SISTERS, BY DEVERIA

nious occasions. The Emperor had endowed his generals and his ministers most liberally, and he required them to spend their money in doing him honor. Therefore, their wives knew that the best way to please the sovereign was to appear in magnificent array, covered with diamonds and precious stones that were used to adorn the great combs then in fashion, or the heavy diadems worn well forward over the forehead, as we see in David's picture of the coronation of the Empress. The Emperor himself paid great attention to the toilette of the court ladies, and while they were still fresh to their new glory and inexperienced in elegance, his Majesty was not chary of reprimands. Even the imperial princesses did not escape reproaches when their toilettes were not thoroughly in harmony with the fête or ceremony which they graced with their presence. The Emperor saw in a color or in a particular kind of trimming a manifestation of criticism or of opposition which existed only in his own imagination. Furthermore, the Empress, the imperial princesses, and the ladies of the court were not prepared by their past habits and education for the important rôle which the course of events and the fortunes of Bonaparte had called upon them to play. Hence the tone of gossip, the frivolity, and the paltry rivalries which characterized the court—rivalries which the emperor himself encouraged, because he preferred to have the ladies concerned with any trifles rather than with politics. The great man withal held women in small esteem, and never hesitated to scold them with a brutality which made Talleyrand say: " What a pity that so great a man is so rude!" (*Quel dommage qu'un si grand homme soit si mal élevé!*). Thus one day he reprimanded the Countess Regnault de Saint-Jean d'Angély in presence of the whole court because he found her too beautiful, and because she eclipsed, in his opinion, another lady in whom for the moment he took a particular interest.

During the Empire the great coiffeur was Michalon, who drove his cabriolet with a negro groom behind, charged a louis for dressing a lady's hair, and was altogether as great a coiffeur as ever lived, and the predecessor of the celebrities of the present day. Indeed, by this time the coiffeur—that is to say, the artist who arranges hair in harmony with physiognomies —was an accepted and necessary institution, having the prestige of a century of existence, and of a profession clearly defined and distinct from that of the barber and the wigmaker, or *perruquier*. This distinction, we may add with a view to excusing a digression which

COUNTESS DE SAINT-JEAN D'ANGÉLY, BY GÉRARD

may be found not unamusing, was established by
a trial in the year 1718, when the corporation of
perruquiers tried to prevent the ladies' coiffeurs
from exercising their newly created trade. On
this occasion Maître Bigot de la Boissière published
a memoir on behalf of the coiffeurs, wherein we
read the following statements, which, though doubtless true enough, will perhaps appear to some mod-
erate minds slightly pretentious and even extravagant:

"We are," says the memoir, "essentially ladies'
hair-dressers, and such functions have secured us
protection; but this protection has made others
jealous, as might have been expected. The bar-
bers and wig-makers have come armed with their
dummy heads, and have been bold enough to pre-
tend that it is their function to dress the hair of
ladies. They have abused certain decrees which do
not apply to our case, and have caused several of
us to be imprisoned. They hold their razors to our
throats, and it is against this tyranny that we are
now obliged to implore the help of Justice." The
memoir then goes on to explain that there is a
wide difference between the trade of the barber
and wig-maker and the talent of dressing ladies'
hair. "The profession of the wig-maker belongs
to the mechanic arts, and that of the ladies' hair-

dresser to the liberal arts. We are neither poets nor painters nor statuaries, but by our special talents we give grace to the beauty which the poet sings; it is often after us that the painter and the statuary represent beauty; and if the hair of Berenice has been placed among the stars, who knows if it did not require our aid in order to arrive at that high degree of glory? The details that our art embraces are infinitely numerous: a forehead more or less large, a face more or less round, demand very different treatment; nature requires always to be embellished or its defects to be repaired; and here the coiffeur must be a painter, familiar with *nuances*, with the use of *chiaro-oscuro*, and with the distribution of light and shade, in order to know how to give more life to the complexion and more expression to the charms. At one time the whiteness of the skin will be relieved by the dark tint of the hair, and the too vivid brilliancy of the blonde will be attenuated by the ashen color that we apply to the hair; the treatment varies in each case according to the different situations. The coiffure for a first meeting is not the same as that for a marriage; and the coiffure for the marriage is different from that for the day after the marriage. The art of dressing the hair of a prude, and of allowing her pretensions to be perceived

MADAME PREVOST, BY GRÉVEDON

without making them obtrusive; the art of displaying the coquette, and of making the mother appear to be the elder sister of the daughter; the art of suiting the coiffure to the affections of the soul which some one is desired to comprehend, to the desire to please, to the languid bearing which wishes only to interest, to the vivacity which will not brook resistance—all this requires an intelligence which is not common and a tact which must be inborn. The art of the coiffeur de dames is therefore an art bordering upon genius, and consequently it is a free and liberal art."

The general opinion is that women were never so badly dressed as they were between the Restoration and the end of the reign of Louis Philippe, and he would indeed be a bold man who would venture to maintain the contrary. Nevertheless, during that epoch which we roughly designate by the conventional date of 1830 there were invented certain coiffures that seem to be not wanting in charm. The general scheme of dressing the hair was a high chignon, generally composed of loops and bows of hair brushed into flat bands, and accompanied by more or less voluminous curls, rolls, shells, loops, or boucles on each side of the temples, the only ornament being flowers or ribbons or a little fichu tied over the

head. Examples are given in our illustrations:
"The Sisters," by Deveria, showing simple curls
and a chignon of loops and braids; the portrait
of the singer, "Madame Prevost," showing more
voluminous curls; and the fancy head, "Marie,"
by Grévedon, being a specimen of a coiffure composed of looped hair, which is certainly not wanting in grace.

In point of fact, a beautiful face is always beautiful, whatever may be the style in which it is
framed, and the art of the epoch in question is by
no means wanting in faces that are beautiful, and
that, too, in a manner peculiarly characteristic of
the times. These were the days of the heroines
of Balzac, the days when Byron, Ossian, and Wal-
ter Scott were à la mode, the days of the Gothic
revival, of Romanticism, and of reminiscences of
chivalry and mediæval sentimentality. Therefore
it is not strange that the ladies of 1830 were ex-
ceedingly romantic, elegiac, plaintive, melting with
tenderness, and full of noble aspirations towards
an ideal which was purely literary and probably
false. They dreamed of pages and châtelaines and
knights-errant; at the same time they allowed
themselves to be compared to Venus, Terpsichore,
Hebe, or Atalanta; and in their gardens they loved
to meditate in a temple of Flora or a grotto dedi-

"MARIE," BY GRÉVEDON

cated to the Naiades over the thrilling pages of the
Vicomte d'Arlincourt's mediæval novel *Le Solitaire*,
the misfortunes of the tender and mysterious Elo-
die, or the pathetic heroes of Madame Delphine
Gay. Above all things, they were mindful of
beauty, in spite of the strange manner in which
they often adorned it; and for this we should be
grateful to them; for, so far as concerns expression and bearing, they were in a way the predecessors of the æsthetic ladies of our own days, inasmuch as their ultimate ideal was inspired by the
literature and the art of the past, by reminiscences
of the age of chivalry and romances of mediæval
princesses—influences which we venture to find as
worthy of respect as the poetry of Rossetti and
the paintings of the pre-Raphaelites. Compared
with the women of the eighteenth century, whose
ideal of beauty was successively frivolous piquancy
and affected ingenuousness, the women of 1830
seem to us infinitely noble and refined, and we can
well understand the admiration which they com-
manded, whether they wore quaintly looped chignons, or drooping ringlets, or crisp side-curls, or
high combs, or simply those flat and sheeny *bandeaux à la Vierge* that frame with contrasting
curves the pure oval of a brunette's face—those
bandeaux which Leonardo da Vinci loved to draw,

and which Perugino used to spend hours in arranging with his own hands on the head of the beautiful girl whom he married when he was already
a graybeard.

All these romantic and sentimental preoccupa-
tions we see depicted in the limpid looks and languishing attitudes of the ladies of this period, in
their unruffled countenances and liquid eyes, in the
satiny smoothness of their glossy curls, in their
expression of calm tenderness and delicacy of soul.
Doubtless the sentimentality of these times was
often ridiculous, and the verses *à la mode* truly
inferior; and yet we may be sure that when these
fair ladies, the image of our grandmothers, were
in the land of the living, their voices rang sweetly
in the ears of men, and that, in the words of Cap-
tain Steele, they were listened to with partiality,
and approbation sat in the countenances of those
with whom they conversed even before they com-
municated what they had to say.

XI

ON JEWELRY AND ORNAMENTS

THE arts of the goldsmith and of the jeweller were born simultaneously. Their history begins at the same moment. As soon as prehistoric man commenced to find pleasure in drawing the profile of an aurochs on the flint of his hatchet, prehistoric woman, we may be sure, was already collecting colored pebbles, boring holes in them, and stringing them into necklaces and ear-rings. The love of ornament seems to be instinctive and incurable. We shall probably delight in personal ornaments to the end of time, and therefore it is good to let the mind dwell upon the subject, with a view to comprehending the why and the wherefore, and thereby intensifying our pleasure.

By jewelry we mean, roughly speaking, personal ornaments of metal with or without the addition of precious stones. Each part of the body has its special jewelry. The head has the crown, the diadem, the fillet, the tænia, hair-pins, aigrettes, combs, frontals, nets, flowers, tiaras, mitres. For the ears

10

and the nose there are rings and droppers. For the neck there are necklaces, collars, carcanets, *pent-à-cols*, lockets, medallions, amulets. For the neck and bosom, to be worn over the garments, are brooches, pins, clasps, fibulæ, breastplates, buttons, pendants, reliquaries, chains, crosses, badges, insignia, and decorations. For the waist there are girdles, buckles, chains, chapelets, châtelaines, escarcelles, and smelling-bottles. For the legs there are rings, anklets, chains, twists, spinthers, pericarps, and dextrals. For the wrists and arms there are bracelets and bands; for the fingers and toes there are rings. For the usages of the toilet there are mirrors and combs and a hundred dainty objects which the art of the jeweller beautifies. There are jewels for all ages and for all sorts and conditions of men, women, and children; there are jewels civil and jewels religious, royal and warlike jewels, jewels sacred and profane, new-fashioned and old-fashioned, and of infinite variety. Jewelry and pottery, such are almost the only relics that remain of the most ancient civilizations. The houses, the vestments, the iron utensils, and the arms of the remote past have returned to dust together with the people who made and used them, but the ornaments have remained. In the museums of Europe and Boulak we see countless specimens of Egyptian jewelry of glass, cut stones, gold, bronze, and enamel. Similar in character and material are the necklaces of glass beads and pendent masks and the gold ornaments of

GOLD WREATH OF MYRTLE LEAVES, ANTIQUE ITALO-GREEK

the Phœnicians, who, according to Castellani, were the inventors of filigree-work. In the museums of Berlin, Athens, and St. Petersburg we see the collections of gold ornaments dug up by Dr. Schliemann in the subsoil of ancient Troy, and the beautiful Greek jewelry discovered in the country of the ancient Scythians, in the mounds of Koul-Aba and Kertch. In the Louvre and the British Museum we can study the marvellous jewelry discovered in recent years in Magna Græcia and Etruria through the intelligent violations of the cemeteries of Vulci, Cervetri, Chiusi, and Toscanella. In various collections are contained specimens of the jewelry of the Assyrians, the Chaldæans, the Persians, the Byzantines, the Moors, the Indians, of the barbarian hordes of the North, and of all the nations of mediæval and modern Europe down to our own times. The materials abound; their co-ordination and historical explanation are merely matters of patience and erudition.

We have not the grave purpose of making a historical study of jewelry, but merely of calling attention to a few examples of beautiful work of the past, with a view to provoking discussion, dissatisfaction, and the spirit of criticism among those who buy and those who wear jewelry; for when we have seen the gold ornaments of the Greeks and the Etruscans, made with 22-carat yellow gold, we are inclined to look with indifference upon the productions of the modern jeweller's art, exception being made of the setting and mounting of precious stones, in which the nineteenth century is

supreme. The sprig of flowers or the branch
of foliage executed in diamonds by contemporary
Parisian artisans is an ornament truly artistic,
and comparable in its way to the beautiful diadems and fibulæ of Athens, and to the splendid
and poetical jewelry of the Renaissance. But our
modern gold ornaments, our necklaces, our ear-
rings, our brooches, how meagre in conception,
how hideous the burnished surface, and how dis-
agreeable the color! What modern brooch or
agrafe can be compared for grace and invention
with an antique Italo-Greek fibula? What modern

TWO FIBULÆ OF BEATEN GOLD, ANTIQUE ITALO-GREEK

diadem surpasses in delicacy of design and work-
manship this wreath of myrtle leaves that once

rested on an Etruscan brow? What ear-rings are
made more dainty than the antique Greek pendants
of winged Victory surmounted
by the solar disk, or Cupids sus-

ANTIQUE ITALO-GREEK EAR-RINGS

pended by fine chains, or the hundreds of designs in filigree and granulated gold of Greek or
Italo-Greek invention? What necklaces are more
sumptuous than those triple and quadruple rows
of pendants, rosettes, and studs hanging from slender hairlike chains that have been found in Etruria
and in the Crimea?

Of late years archæologists have begun to use the
word Etruscan very carefully when speaking of objects of art, and to prefer the less compromising
term Italo-Greek, for in reality we know very lit-

tle about Etruscan art beyond the fact that it is
obviously a more or less original combination of
Oriental and Hellenic elements. In the earlier
Etruscan art the Oriental influence is supreme; in
the later art the Hellenic influence reigns unrival-
led. But how was the primitive Oriental influence
exercised? Who were the intermediaries between
the East and central Italy, where the Etruscans existed in the form of a great
political confederation as early
as the tenth century B.C.? Were
the Etruscans colonists from
Asia Minor? If this hypothesis be not true, how does it
happen that we find the same
system of burial in Etruria and
in Asia Minor? Why do the
Etruscans alone of the Medi-
terranean peoples practise the
art of divination? Why do
they wear Oriental costume —
long flowered robes with brilliantly colored borders, Lydian
sandals, and hoods that remind
one of the Phrygian bonnet?
Why are the Etruscan games and amusements of
Lydian origin? All these questions the archæolo-

ANTIQUE ITALO-GREEK
EAR-RING

gists ask with a desire to find confirmation of the legend of the Lydian emigration under Tyrrhenos, which Herodotus has recorded, and which Virgil has embellished.

On the other hand, although an Asiatic migration into Etruria cannot be absolutely demonstrated, the commercial relations between Etruria and the East are indisputable, and the intermediaries were the Phœnicians. The Etruscans, through the Phœnicians, were in commercial relations with Carthage, Egypt, Greece, and the East. Their markets were supplied with all the products of the East — gold, silver, ivory, precious stones, purple, jewelry, caskets, decorated ceramics, imitation Assyrian and Egyptian wares. These objects of Asiatic style were used as models by the native Etruscan workmen for the manufacture of bronze utensils, jewelry, and rings, and thus the most ancient objects of art of Etruscan origin are decorated exclusively with Eastern designs — roses, palms, lotus flowers, lions, tigers, panthers, fantastic animals, sphinxes, griffins, winged bulls. Even during the Roman epoch the Etruscans continued to employ Eastern *motifs* and patterns to decorate mirrors and cinerary urns, to compose frames for paintings, handles and feet for vases, and ornaments for furniture and all kinds of utensils. These Oriental *motifs* became so usual that they passed into the traditions of Roman art, and thence, at the time of the Renaissance, into modern art, where they continue to constitute one of the chief resources of our silversmiths, jewellers, potters, and wood-carvers.

As for the Hellenic influence in Etruria, it is evidently very ancient, for it is certain that Hellenic emigration into Italy began long before the historic period, while the commercial relations which this emigration established gradually developed century after century, until the Hellenic influence became preponderating. The great objects of commerce were pottery, painted vases, and gold jewelry. The immense majority of the so-called Etruscan vases were indisputably manufactured in Greece, and there is every reason to believe that the most beautiful and elegant specimens of that gold jewelry which we call Etruscan were made not by native artists, but by the Greeks, who, alone of the ancients, had taste so exquisite that they never sacrificed beauty of form to profusion of detail or exuberance of fanciful decoration.

Meanwhile this antique Greek or Italo-Greek jewelry remains masterly, and in certain details of delicate manipulation inimitable. The process of manufacture is not chasing, chisel-work, stamping, or moulding, but soldering and superposition. This, according to Castellani, is the reason why the gold ornaments of the ancients have so marked a character, deriving their distinction from the spontaneous idea and inspiration of the artist, rather than from the cold and regular execution of the workman. The very imperfections and voluntary neglect of certain parts give to antique jewelry an artistic appearance that we seek for in vain in most modern work, which is unisome in aspect, commonplace, and wanting in *inti-* *mité*. Then again

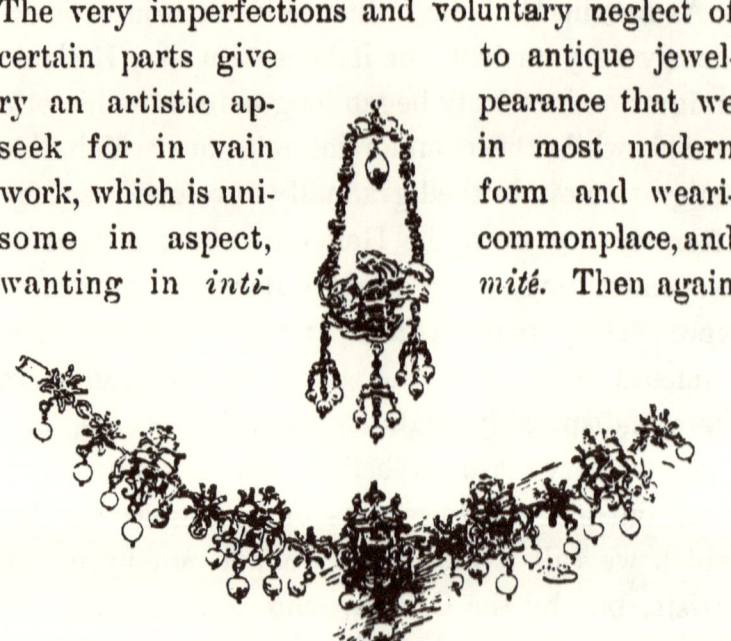

RENAISSANCE PENDANT AND BRACELET

the gold ornaments of antiquity are more charming and brilliant to the eye than modern work because the matter employed is different. The ancients, like the artists of the Renaissance, used gold 22 carats fine, only two parts of alloy,

just sufficient to give the resistance and durability
which absolutely pure gold does not possess, and
yet not enough to impair the brilliancy of the
precious metal. Gold of 22 carats is not oxidizable, and does not blacken in the fire. It remains of a fine yellow color, which improves with
wear, and needs no polishing. Its beauty resides
in the substance itself, which is unchangeable.
Gold of this quality is perfectly malleable, and
receives enamels of all kinds without changing
their color or lessening their transparency. The
gold employed by modern jewellers is 18 carats
fine; it is slightly oxidizable; it changes the color
of certain enamels; under the action of fire the
surface becomes covered with copper oxides, which
need to be removed by scraping, and then the object has to be polished with pumice, tripoli, and
rouge, or else colored yellow by immersion in baths
of salts and acids. The artificial coloring and pol-
ish thus obtained disappear with wear, and the object becomes more or less hideous, whereas the
22-carat yellow gold improves with age. It may,
however, be asked whether the average modern
eye is sufficiently educated to appreciate the beauty
of the color of gold and the fine shades of tone in
transparent enamel.

In the massive jewelry of the Middle Ages the

MIRROR-CASE, FOURTEENTH CENTURY, FRENCH

modern woman will perhaps find but few suggest-
ions for elegance. On the other hand, in the toilet accessories of that epoch there are many examples worthy of imitation, at least so far as the
spirit is concerned. The collections of the Louvre,
the British Museum, South Kensington, and the
museums of Italy and Germany are very rich in

toilet articles of ivory and boxwood, which well repay a passing glance. The ivory mirror-cases are always most elaborately carved, generally with scenes of chivalry and love. In the South Kensington Museum one mirror-case represents four mounted knights fighting at the foot of a battlemented tower, from the top of which three maidens pelt them with roses. Another represents the castle of Love besieged by mounted knights, who

SIXTEENTH CENTURY COMB, FRENCH

climb up the towers with rope-ladders and elope with willing ladies. Other mirror-cases in the British Museum are adorned with representations of the storming of the castle of Love, hunting-par-

ties where the ladies with hawks on their fists ride
side by side with their lords, scenes of courtship,
concerts, serenades, the stories of Lucretia and of
Pyramus and Thisbe, the Nativity, the adoration

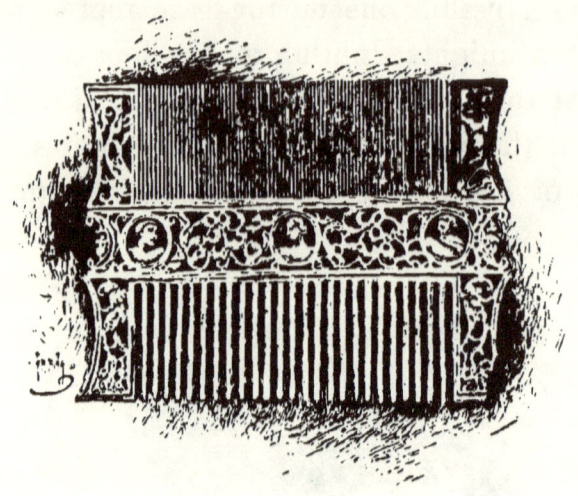

SIXTEENTH CENTURY COMB, ITALIAN

of the Magi, etc. Mediæval combs are also carved
with similar subjects. One comb in the South
Kensington collection represents a concert, and
men and women dancing; another comb of the
beginning of the sixteenth century is adorned with
a scene which appears to be the judgment of
Paris; another very beautiful Italian comb of the
same date is ornamented with arabesque scroll-
work and medallions enclosing busts. We may
safely affirm that no lady of the present day combs

her hair with such an exquisitely artistic comb as this one.

Several specimens of the jewelry and ornaments of the time of the Renaissance have been noticed incidentally in previous pages, notably in connection with the portraits of the two daughters of Charles V. and of the Duchess of Urbino. At the moment when the rediscovery of antiquity produced that splendid movement of art and thought which we call the Renaissance there existed three schools of jewellers whose works are known to us chiefly through the monuments of painting and sculpture. The Flemish painters have depicted for us the jewelry of Bruges and Ghent; the primitive painters of Italy show us the jewelry of Sienna and Florence; and the mediæval sculptors have preserved the types of the jewelry of old France. The triumph of the Renaissance spirit in Italy, and the spread of Italian influence all over Europe, put an end to the personality of these local schools, and brought into vogue the style to which we give the name of Renaissance—a style created by the independent efforts of many great men, but yet strongly impressed with certain common characteristics. In the days of the Renaissance the great designers of jewelry were Mantegna and Michael Angelo, Ghirlandajo and Pollajuolo, Francia and

Verrocchio, Benvenuto Cellini and Leonardo, Albert Dürer and Jean Cousin; for at that time the great artists were universal, and the painter did not think it undignified to design a brooch or the sculptor to model a salt-cellar. The artists of the Renaissance were, however, unacquainted with actual specimens of antique jewelry, no objects of importance having been found until the excavations of the present century in Etruria and the Crimea. They were therefore saved from the danger of imitation, and left without guide or model to apply to decorative purposes the materials which the newly discovered literature and art of pagan antiquity placed at their disposal. Thus we find the jewelry of the Renaissance ornamented with figures of gods, fauns, satyrs, and grotesque figures

RENAISSANCE PENDANT

of mythological inspiration, engraved in stones, chased on gold, cast, repoussé, and enamelled; for it was especially in the art of chiselling and enamelling that the artists of the Renaissance excelled.

The Renaissance pendants are peculiarly characteristic, and a fine specimen is the merman reproduced
in our illustration, made of a baroque pearl, with

THE MERMAN

hanging pearls mounted in gold, and enriched with
precious stones and colored enamels most ingeniously disposed. Very beautiful, too, are the Renaissance pendants of regular design, and the rich
bracelets and magnificent ceintures and chains of
beautifully wrought gold embellished with colored
enamel and gems. But of beautiful jewelry we
might give countless examples were the number of

11

our illustrations unlimited, and were we sure of not fatiguing the attention of the reader by the reiteration of views which are perhaps too completely opposed to current contemporary ideas. Thanks doubtless to atavism or mysteriously innate Oriental prejudices, the writer of these vain pages takes no interest in the programmes and results of universities for women. Vassar laureates and Girton graduates are indifferent to him. IIis conviction is that for a woman gifted with beauty the ideal occupation is to wear beautiful clothes and ornaments, and look charming. IIe would fain see women loaded with jewelry like idols, with diadems and ear-plates on their heads, long droppers in their ears, their bosoms glittering with necklaces, their waists encircled with girdles of glory, their arms stiff with bracelets, and their ankles bedecked with rings that would jingle as they walked. Evidently this ideal cannot be realized in the actual conditions of Occidental life, with its lack of privacy and modesty, its brusqueness of movement and gesture, its haste and unquietness in all things. Therefore it is useless to pursue further these fragmentary studies of jewelry and feminine adornments, the more so as the Renaissance was soon blighted by the Reformation, since which event the adornment of beauty has been tolerated at the best rather than frankly commended and encouraged. Nevertheless, women continue to be beautiful, and there are at the present day thousands and thousands of ladies who dress divinely; but, with the exception of the Arab women of the Ouled Naïl tribe and the Nautch girls of India, no modern woman wears enough jewelry and ornaments of gold. For that reason we have been obliged to limit our admiration to the pictures and statues of the past, and to enjoy in imagination what the meanness of the age refuses to the desire of the eyes.

THE END

By THEODORE CHILD

ART AND CRITICISM. Monographs and Studies. Richly Illustrated. Large 8vo, Cloth, Ornamental, Uncut Edges and Gilt
Top, $6 oo. (*In a Box.*)

A MIRROR OF FAIR WOMEN. Japan Edition. Complete in
Seven Parts. Edition Limited to One Thousand Numbered and
Registered Copies. (*Sold only by subscription.*)

THE PRAISE OF PARIS. Illustrated. 8vo, Cloth, Ornamental, $2 50.

THE SPANISH-AMERICAN REPUBLICS. Profusely Illus-
trated by T. DE THULSTRUP, FREDERIC REMINGTON, WILLIAM
HAMILTON GIBSON, W. A. ROGERS, and other eminent artists.
Large 8vo, Cloth, Ornamental, $3 50.

THE TSAR AND HIS PEOPLE; or, Social Life in Russia. By
THEODORE CHILD, EUGÈNE MELCHOIR DE VOGÜÉ, and Others.
Profusely Illustrated. Square 8vo, Cloth, Uncut Edges and Gilt
Top, $3 oo.

SUMMER HOLIDAYS. Post 8vo, Cloth, Ornamental, $1 25.

DELICATE FEASTING. Post 8vo, Cloth, Ornamental, $1 25.

PUBLISHED BY HARPER & BROTHERS, NEW YORK

☞ *The above works are for sale by all booksellers, or will be sent by mail,
postage prepaid, to any part of the United States, Canada, or Mexico, on
receipt of the price.*

www.ingramcontent.com/pod-product-compliance
Lightning Source LLC
Chambersburg PA
CBHW030128030726
47498CB00007B/2601